Golden Days in Donegal

Stephen Joyce

INISHSCOT
Publications
Glasgow & Inishowen

Golden Days in Donegal

Golden days in Donegal was first published by InishScot Publications in 2005.

The author and publisher are indebted to *IRDL* for their support in the publication of this book as part of their cultural awards scheme.

Scottish Address:
InishScot Publications, 31 Dunvegan Drive, Glasgow, G64 3LB, Scotland, U.K.

Irish Address:
InishScot Publications, 6 Foyle Haven, James Street, Moville, Co. Donegal, Ireland.

ISBN   0-9550703-0-9

Design and Lay Out: Stephen Toye
Printing: Browne Printers, Letterkenny, Co. Donegal, Ireland.

The author and publisher are indebted to *The Inish Times* and *The Derry Journal* for the colour photographs in the book.

A percentage of any profits from the sale of the book will go to support the work of *SOLAS* who respond to the needs of Inishowen children with Dyslexia - and their families.

Volume One

MEMORIES

Memories light the corners of my mind
Memories, golden memories,
of the way things were.

Was it all so different then
Or
has time re-written every line?
If we had to do it all again,
Would we?
Could we?

Introduction: *Voices from Inishowen*

I have written this book from outside of Inishowen , from another country, and tried to look back in time to recall the beautiful memories of my childhood summer holidays. But the book is not about me – it is about the people of Inishowen – past and present. and the joy they brought to my life. As the book took shape , my recollections of people and events have been greatly enhanced by the thoughts , recollections and support of Inishowen folk of today – family and friends - old and new .

In particular, I am privileged to include the comments and words of the following Inishowen authors an introduction to the book for you . They have all inspired me to continue to write down my memories and have supported me at different times in their own invaluable ways.

Sean Beattie

The waters of Lough Foyle flow calmly through this memoir.
As the Scotch boat sails up The Foyle, its passengers know a warm welcome awaits them on arrival at their destination. Stephen recalls for us some of the memories of summer days in Donegal half a century ago. There was haymaking on warm summer days in the meadow below the house; horses carted turf home from the bog for winter fuel and thatchers could be seen at work on the roofs of whitewashed cottages. There were acres of potatoes growing in every townland and fields of corn were thriving on every farm. It was all a slower pace of life, but Stephen Joyce reminds us that it was lived to the full. As he has suggested in his title, it was a golden time.

Hazel McIntyre

Stephen Joyce's warm , vivid account of his memories of Donegal will be treasured by all who read it. Stephen's personal narrative provides an unrivalled insight into the lives and social history of his beloved Inishowen.

Jimmy McBride

I am so pleased that you contacted me about the songs that you recollected from your youth, and that I was in a position to be of assistance to you in your quest. I was doubly delighted that you had, after all these years, remembered them and the ghaeilge and that you thought it worthwhile to include samples of your enthusiasm for the language in your writings.

I eagerly await this publication that will , I am certain, strengthen the bonds that exist between our common Celtic Heritage.

A'dh mor ar do shaothar agus ar do chuid oibre

Good luck in your work and in your endeavours

Evelyn Ruddy

Stephen Joyce's book about visits to his native Rooskey will jog the memory of many people from Inishowen and the North West who emigrated to Glasgow in the late 40's and 50's. The close ties that existed between Glasgow and Donegal are emphasised as many Scots - or ' Scotchies' as they were referred to here in Inishowen , spent the Glasgow Holidays in Donegal.

As recalled in Stephen's book, they stayed with friends and relatives – or else in the boarding houses and guest houses of that period. Many people in Donegal will recall the excitement which the arrival of these visitors generated. This book will also give younger people an insight into a lifestyle far removed from today, and , hopefully will encourage older people to record their memories of an age that has virtually disappeared.

WELCOME TO MY WORLD

Welcome to my world,
won't you come on in ?
Miracles I guess, still happen now and then.
Step into my world,
Leave your cares behind !
Welcome to my world,
It's built with you in mind.

Failte go mo shaol –sa,
tarraing ort isteach ?
Silim nach d'tarlaionn na miorbhailt ach anois ' s aris.
Siul isteach i mo shaol – sa
agus fag triobloid ' do dhiaidh.
Failte go mo shaol –sa
Ta se togtha ' gus tisa I gceist

Jim Reeves No. 1 Pop song of the 1950's

Stephen, sister Bridget, uncle Johnnie, aunt Liza and Stephen's mum and dad
outside his Donegal cottage. The family joy at being back in Inishowen is obvious.

Golden Days in Donegal

Golden days in Donegal is dedicated to the memory of my mother and father, it is a nostalgic journey back in time as I try to recall and share the magic of my school holidays in Donegal in the 1950's. The book was inspired by a recent visit I made to RUSKEY, Quigley's Point – to the cottage where I was born over half a century ago.

Like so many of us who return, I was stunned to see the cottage lying derelict. As I struggled through the weeds and undergrowth, I forced my way in through the old kitchen window. As the memories came flooding back of the people I had shared so much with – laughter, songs and stories – I searched about - trying to find any mementoes of the golden days which had gone forever. To my sheer delight, in the ruins of the lower bedroom, where the floorboards had rotted away, I found an old school jotter - wrapped up in a Daniel Doherty's bread wrapper.

I remembered using the jotter as a diary to jot down notes on the events of 1955 and on the precious people and places of my holidays. Some of what I had written down was still readable and I have included what I could. I would like to share these memories with you and try to recapture those golden days with you. There are no momentous world events in the book. I have simply tried to be as accurate as I could in what I have written down and tried to remember the very best of those golden days. The book is all about the everyday people and happenings of life in Donegal as I saw them half a century ago. It is about a young boy's attempts to feel a sense of belonging to the place where he was born and to express his love of his Irish heritage and culture.

To me and my family, all the people we shared our lives with then were important - and through them I hope we can take a nostalgic look back at a way of life which has almost disappeared and which too easily can be demeaned.

In sharing these memories with you, I would like to thank the following people for inspiring me and supporting me in what proved to be a much more difficult task than I thought. It is not easy to recall and put down everyday incidents and stories of long ago with accuracy and with due respect to the people who were at the centre of my Donegal World. As I was recalling these ordinary events for the book, I was only too aware that the people in the book who brought such enrichment to our lives, had still to deal everyday with their own family and personal worries, tragedies and struggles. Despite of all these, they brought sunshine into the lives of so many of us by their affection, friendships and love. Without them, the book would have been impossible to write and I dedicate it especially to them.

The task of sharing these recollections with you was also only made possible with the involvement of the following people, to whom I am eternally grateful.

- *Ann and my own family*
- *Bridget, John and Martin Joyce*
- *Nicola Moir, Greencastle, Inishowen* (Student at Moville Community School)
- *Patricia Ferns from Dalefern Travel, Glasgow*

On a professional level, I am privileged to have recently read and been motivated by the books of Sean Beattie, Hazel McIntyre, Evelyn Ruddy, John A. McLaughlin and Jimmy McBride.

Each of these writers gave me their full personal support and specialist knowledge at the most important times in the book's completion.

I would also like to give a special thanks to Gerard Duddy at Moville Library who first introduced me to these wonderful Inishowen writers. He was always there when I needed information on local history and culture and willingly made the Donegal library services available to me to support my writing.

In particular, I was inspired recently by John A. McLaughlin's excellent book 'Carrowmenagh - History of a Donegal Village and Townland '. In John's book , Bishop Edward Daly wrote :

'I hope that other individuals will embark on similar projects on their own townlands.'

My own hope is that ' Golden Days in Donegal ' is a credit to Bishop Daly's invitation and can help to encourage others to continue to preserve the history, culture and heritage of our beautiful Inishowen.

To all of them, all I can say is:
Go raibh mile maith agat

Stephen Joyce

CONTENTS

Chapter 1

Dawn on the Foyle

It is dawn. It is June 30th. It is 1955. Fifty years ago - and a million years ago in memories. Fifty long years since the Lairds Loch swung round the Antrim Coast that day, taking me back again into the Foyle and up to Derry. Taking my mother, brother John, sister Bridget and myself back to Inishowen, so that we could once again head down the road past Culmore, through the customs at Muff, into Quigley's Point and then on to the Ruskey Road at Whitecastle.

'John' I shouted to my brother as I held up our old pair of binoculars to him.

'We're nearly there. I can see the Foyle. I can see Portrush and over there to our right – I think it's Kinnagoe Bay - and look! I think I can see Shroove beach.'

But my brother John, my mother and my sister Bridget were all still half asleep and had put up with numerous false alarms and false sightings of the hills of Inishowen - ever since we had skirted the edge of the Antrim coast in the early hours of the dawn.

It had indeed been a long night - a long, glorious, chaotic and magical night.

It was almost 12 hours now since our eldest brother Paddy had seen us safely off from our tenement home near Maryhill Barracks in Glasgow. With our dad out all hours working on building sites to bring in enough to pay the bills, it was Paddy who was always there, looking after us, organising sailing tickets and buses or taxis and making sure that we got away safely on our Summer break. He knew that my mother, just recovering from major surgery, needed the healthy air and quiet life of her own Inishowen cottage.

Paddy, the first in our family, was admired by all of us, and especially the old people back in Dongeal where he had spend so many of his own schoolboy holidays, almost becoming adopted by my mother's parents, so much they loved his quiet, caring nature. But now he was there as always on the quayside - waving, before heading back to his own shiftwork as the Lairds

Loch cast off. As we looked back and waved fondly to him, we all knew our dad would be proud that Paddy had taken all that burden off him and set us out on our journey back to the Inishowen hills and people we all loved.

We knew Paddy and our dad were with us in spirit as the Lairds Loch slowly made her joyous, relentless way down the river Clyde - past the clattering shipyards - down past crowds waving from the shore at Anderston, Clydebank, Dumbarton and Greenock - and then picked up speed as she headed confidently out into the Irish Sea.

But the chaos and noise and lack of sleep had been swept away as we passed Paddy's Milestone and our Irish songs rang out and the children laughed and the adults reminisced. And we all sang and danced and endlessly wandered around the ship in an ecstasy of fascination and delight. As the strains of *Carn Fair* and *Danny Boy* and *The Hills of Donegal* drifted out from the ship and across the waters towards the disappearing Scottish Coast, we were in a kind of time warp.

Our minds blotted out all the frantic, last – minute rushing, just to get the money for the trip. All the hurried packing was forgotten and the dash to the Broomielaw on Clyde Street. Then the wait and our shuffling through the noisy, twisting queue to get up the ramp and onto the ship. Then our hasty search for lifejackets to use as pillows on the best wooden seats we could find to use as our beds throughout the night.

And as the night closed in and the sounds of the singing and the laughter and the tears died down, our eager eyes glanced out the portholes a thousand times. As sleep came and went we took eager turns to catch the first glimpses of the outline of the Irish Coast.

And now we were nearly there. As the sun broke out and the early morning mist vanished and the boat's relentless bow wave took us ever and ever closer to the Foyle, my heart raced and I had to get everyone up and ready.

I knew (and they knew) that it would be an hour, maybe nearly two, before we eased past Culmore lighthouse. But this was the one part of our journey home that we would relish and savour as every minute passed and every eye scanned the coastline for familiar sights and sounds. With the white glimmering outlines of Portrush and Portstewart fading behind us on our left, we saw the dazzling Magilligan sands come into view.

I eagerly carried a large cup of tea to my mother who gently encouraged us to go on with our excited preparations to get upstairs and savour dawn on the Foyle - and the sights and sounds of our first Inishowen morning. We shook off our night tiredness, quickly gathered our belongings as if we were just about to disembark in minutes - and clambered up the double rows of stairs to catch our first glimpse of Moville.

I can still remember that first view of its long white wall, weaving and twisting along the Green. Then the church spires and every now and again the drifting ribbons of smoke, as fires were lit and the cold wind of dawn started to bring life, not just to us on the ship, but to the families and friends and shopkeepers on our Inishowen coast.

Tiny punts chugged their way back across the Foyle after their night's fishing, desperate to get to their shelters in Greencastle before they were caught up in the swell of the ship as she moved steadily up the Foyle and past the Moville light. We thought we could recognise faces in the bobbing boats - Willie John, Packie Jo, Mickey and Phelim, but it was probably just our imagination that we thought we knew every face and every tiny landmark in that early morning light.

But now, up on the Inishowen hills to our right we could see beyond the Redcastle light and up towards Whitecastle with its solid, sentinel house on the shore – a relic of our ancestors the McLaughlins who had fought their battles and won their lands there centuries before. I now trained my my old binoculars on the patchwork of criss -cross fields just beyond Drung and up towards Ruskey.

I thought of the fire being lit in uncle Johnnie's cottage and could make out the row of sheets flapping their welcome along the rodden which ran along the field in front of the house. And then I made out the smoke drifting up from the chimney of the small thatched cottage in which I was born and my mother and my mother's father. I took a deep, deep breath.

We were trying to take in everything now and savouring every moment, hoping that somehow we could stop time and keep these moments for ever. As the sun rose higher, the fields seemed closer, the fires were lit and our destination of Derry grew close. In the hurly burly of crowded decks now, we were past Quigley's Point and the Greenbank Hall and up facing Ture. Ahead of us, as we cast furtive, last glances back down the Foyle, we could see the narrowing of the river and the lighthouse at Culmore.

Gently the ship slowed and eased through the narrows and, as she swung towards the quay, we could see the towers and the spires of Derry and the narrow, cobbled slanting rows of streets running up from the waterfront. We made our way along the deck - exhilarated and exhausted – trying to gain the best positions to get off the boat quickly and make our way to Great James Street for the bus if my mother's cousin Neil Smith wasn't on the quayside to meet us.

As the Lairds Loch swung round at the quayside to face down the river again, I gazed in awe at the silent, unknown, timeless men who grasped the ropes in their roughened hands, ready to use them to pull over the long, thick cable ropes that would tie our ship to the quay. Then suddenly with a thud we were moored at the Derry quay and we struggled and half stumbled down the gangways with our luggage. We hoped on hope that Neil Smith, my mother's favourite cousin, would be there from Drung to meet us. We were prepared though that Neil wouldn't be there - and wasn't able make it this time - maybe had been out salmon fishing or had a better hire. If he wasn't there, we knew and were ready to happily drag our cases along the quayside, up past the Diamond and along to Great James street for the first bus to Moville.

So, the first magical part of our journey was now over. We were safely in Derry in the stillness of the early dawn as the city roused itself again. That first year, no car had come, so we waited anxiously but exhilarated until the first bus at 7.55 trundled into the street and we slumped down on our seats and headed down the road towards Moville.

The journey out of Derry always roused us from any tiredeness as we knew we were now heading out of the silent city and down towards the customs Posts. There was no need to stop and Dannie the driver on that day swept the bus round the bend and through the main street at Muff. We waved as people stirred in the early morning sun and we now felt that everything was different; the roads, the signs, the whole landscape. As the bus raced down past Ture and through Greencastle, we tried to control our excitement as we began to count the minutes until we would see the Whitecastle gates and know that we were nearly there.

Danny eased the bus in to the left at the foot of the Ruskey Road and we ushered our mother to the open door and helped her down the bus steps. We eagerly unloaded our bags and cases, and as we stood back from the bus and waved to the passengers who were heading on down the road, we knew that we had finished the first stage of our journey. It was a wonderful feeling inside each of us that we were now about to spend our Summer holidays among the Inishowen hills and the people of Donegal we loved so much.

The silence was deafening as the noise of the bus faded down the road towards Drung, and we all sat down at the foot of the road for my mother to double check that we had all our bags and cases and were ready for the long but glorious trek up the steep, first slope of the Ruskey Road. Then, it was on and upwards until we reached my godmother Bridget's cottage and we could take a final rest before we mounted the brow of the Ruskey brae.

My brother John was always away ahead of the rest of us, leading the way and moving round the small bends in the road out of our sight, checking and hoping that someone might be on their way down the road to meet us at that early hour. Every few minutes we would hear him shouting:

'We're nearly there. Nearly there mum. It's just another slope and then ... I can see Barr's. Yes... its Barr's and we're almost there! I think I can see someone like Uncle Johnnie up there just below Bridget's. I think he's coming down to meet us.'

At that John threw off his bag and raced back down towards us. He swiftly took two other brown bags from my mother and raced back up to where he had dropped his own. As he laid them down, we could just make him out waving up the road and jumping up to make sure that our Uncle Johnnie knew it was us.

Uncle Johnnie leads Nellie and her family up to the fields at the start of the day.
As the Lairds Loch sailed up the Foyle, he was already getting on with his daily chores.

But Uncle Johnnie had already been up for over two hours and had lit the turf fire and let his hens out and done a hundred other minor tasks around the cottage. Our Aunt Liza with her sharp ears had heard in the silence of the hills the low, echoing sound of the engine whining its relentless way down towards Moville.

It was Liza who had let Johnnie know and he had thrown on some of his best clothes to come down the road and meet my mother, his young sister Mary. It was an important and happy short journey for him this time as my mother had been in hospital for over a year with TB. At that time there were no advanced drugs and she had undergone major surgery and fought back twice when the odds were all against her and the hospital had sent twice for my father to prepare him for the worst.

In the thatched cottage in which she had been born and to which we were heading, Johnnie and Liza had only the slightest idea of the dark days when my mother lay at death's door in Robroyston Hospital. Nor had they had any word about the numerous police calls at our Maryhill house for my father to rush by tramcar and bus in response to an urgent message from the hospital that my mum was not likely to pull through.

But all that was forgotten as my Uncle Johnnie clasped his sister and quickly slung half the bags over his eager shoulders. As usual, Uncle Johnnie had known more than we thought and his family instinct had kept the worry hidden in his mind, despite the miles they were apart.

'Time to get you all home, Mary. Liza's got the kettle on and you can take it easy now for a few weeks. Boys O Boys! Mary.... There were too many times this year when we thought we'd never see you coming up the Ruskey Brae again!"

-

Diary : July 1st 1955

First Night in Ruskey!

Brilliant!

Left Glasgow at 6 yesterday.

Arrived 8 this morning.

Sailing on Lairds Loch fantastic.

Magical night. Singing, Talking

and walking round boat.

SAW Ayshire lights AND Paddy's Milestone (Ailsa Craig)

BUS had no problems coming down through Muff.

Remember Mammy searched last year.

Rushed down to see Kathleen and Philomena Barr.

LOVELY TEA & SCONES in HAYFIELD.

SAW James's new horse (Nelly?)

HOME AT LAST!

REMEMBER!!!

Ask Uncle Johnnie about Irish words

for Daddy coming over at Glasgow Fair!

Chapter 2

In The Black of Night

O ne of the things I found most difficult to adjust to at the start of our Donegal holidays was the sudden and utter darkness which came down on us when night fell.

Back in Glasgow we never really knew what sheer black night was. My mother and father had often told us about the need for blackouts during the Second World War, still fresh in their memory. Although they had both been brought up in the Irish countryside – my mother in Donegal and my father in the hills near Leenane in Galway – they had soon to face the nightmare of the German bombings on Glasgow. They had had to endure the long, dark nights of terror in the air-raid shelters in the knowledge that one slender chink of light from a slit curtain or crack could alert enemy bombers to come down with a vengeance on any easy target.

We could never understand how a little slit of light coming from a window could be so life threatening, but when we heard their graphic account of the ferocious and deadly bombing of a nearby street, Kilmun Street, we got their message. We soon learned as very young children that our Glasgow home was right beside the prime target of Maryhill Barracks and that all our lives could have been snuffed out in seconds by a careless shaft of light.

In fact they told us that the terrible destruction that hit Kilmun street that night of the Marythill blitz had been caused when a careless neighbour, having had too much to drink, left the blind up on his kitchen window. Before the local police or air-raid wardens could see the light from the window, the sirens had gone for the raid and a German bomber at the head of a large formation spotted the flickering light from Tam's kitchen. It was disastrous, as the pilot instantly gave the bearings of the houses to the other bombers and Kilmun Street was raised to the ground with over 30 families wiped out.

But as we grew up in in Glasgow during the post – war years, thoughts and memories of blackouts faded away. In our neighbourhoods, lights were an everyday part of city life – on the landings of our tenement closes – on the stairs, outside our close and on the corners of our streets.

Lights were everywhere and when the weather permitted we played at games in the closes and lanes and at football till well after dusk - dribbling, tackling and scoring glorious goals under the ever present glare of the street lights. Even right outside our front bedroom, the street light was always on and although we drew the curtains and this dimmed the light from the street, there was never any sense of real darkness, even in the long winter nights.

It was all so different as we began to settle into our holiday cottage in the hills and adjust to the excitement and strangeness of our new environment. I remember that it took my eyes a long number of nights to get used to the sudden and utter blackness when Aunt Liza decided that the Tillie Lamp on the kitchen table was to go out. There was never any discussion about what time it should go out or what was to happen if you weren't tired enough to go to bed - or if we were out visiting, down at Yankee Bridgets or at Kathleen and Philomena Barr's house or at Mary Rose Armstrong's.

Liza, in her economical and no – nonsense way, would dim and then extinguish the Tillie Lamp completely in a swift and flamboyant movement of the hand. She would swiftly slip off the glass lamp, take a deep exaggerated breath and snuff out the flame on the wick in a instant – whether you were in the house or not !

On the first few nights before we started to stay out later and go round the houses till early dawn, the sudden and sheer blackness of the dark was staggering. It was if a wall of black suddenly came down all around you. If you weren't already in bed, you had to feel your way uneasily along from the dying turf fire, using its shadowy light to guide you into the darkened lower room.

Once in the lower room, it was a slow and stumbling shuffle past the dressing table and the glass washing bowl on top of it, across the cold floor, fumbling for the bedposts and the soft straw hay mattresses and into the warmth and security of the big bed.

Liza liked the doors closed between the kitchen and the bedroom as she always seemed to have urgent matters to discuss with Uncle Johnnie. Sometimes, as we lay transfixed in the dark, we could hear them talking about bringing in the hay or about a sick animal. At other times, in whispers, it was about uncle Johnnie having to do something drastic about the fox that was using the curtain of darkness to try its best to empty the hen house.

We found then in the darkness of the room where you could hold your hand out and not be able to see it, that we had security in numbers and voices. As we snuggled down into the soft straw beds, we kept up a constant, excited whispered chatter about our own events of the day and regularly asking each other naively if we were still there in the bed.

My mother, at the upper end of the bed tried in vain often to shoosh us to be quiet, but we knew that she, thinking nothing of the pitch black in the room, would sympathetically ignore the whispered stories, questions, tales and adventures we shared, trying to pretend that the darkness didn't matter.

However, once the darkness was total and my brothers' and sister's tired voices began to fade off into sleep. I often remember lying there trying to see my hand in front of my face. It was a scary and bewildering feeling that you knew your hand was almost touching your nose, but you couldn't see it at all – or anything else until the first soft touches of dawn light began to appear.

In the total darkness I remember trying to orientate myself. I tried to work out where things were in the lower room : the unlit fireplace to the right of my head at the top of the bed, the dressing table and wash up basin over near where I knew the window should be and most important of all, the door out into the kitchen. It was re -assuring to know that it was there -almost directly facing me as I lay still, thinking and then trying to doze off with the others. The last thing I wanted was to suddenly realise that I was the only one awake - and aware of the pitch blackness and the still, utterly silent room.

Getting used to the blackness was a strange experience until the first nights passed and we got somewhat used to it, but we never felt in any danger, despite our unease at being in total darkness. It was so different from being back in Glasgow where, if any sudden noise or voice outside was heard in the darkness, we would have been jumping up and running to switch on a light in fear.

It took us a number of nights to settle and relax and accept that, unlike Glasgow there was no danger of burglars or thieves lurking about to scale up ronepipes if they thought a window was open and the people in the house were fast asleep.

Of course the darkness was used as a great opportunity for my brother John to re -tell the stories of goblins and witches and banshees that Aunt Liza so regularly filled our minds with round the turf fire as the night drew in. It seemed so easy to listen and enjoy her scary tales while we were all together. It seemed so safe in the light of the Tillie Lamp and with a huge turf fire lighting up around the cottage walls. We were so captivated then and so brave and never glanced behind us in fear or anxiety.

What a difference if we were in bed in the total darkness and silence. John would suddenly and quietly in his dramatic, eerie voice recall the terrors and the ghoulish deaths which we had sat back and listened to earlier with a shrug or a laugh or a silent nod.

But John understood our fear of the dark and waited until the room became pitch black and knew that we were unsettled and still adjusting to the Inishowen nights. Then to our continuous mixture of terror and pleasure he would recall in vivid, scary detail, all the horrible events of the headless rider from Cabry, maybe calling outside our cottage that night to end his nightmare journey. Then, in a chilling, whistling voce, John would remind us of the muffled, plaintif call of the Whitecastle Ghost who wandered the lower fields above the Foyle, in a never-ending aimless search for his only child who had drowned in the river across at the mossy glen.

Diary : July 3rd 1955

DARK DARK night last night.
Nothing like Glasgow.
Aunt Liza put out Tillie Lamp before we got to bed.
Black as coal.
I couldn't see my hand in front of me.
John scared us with Ghost stories about Redcastle.

NOTES:
Started learning Irish words.
I want to learn them for daddy coming over in two weeks at
Glasgow Fair.

Here's my FIRST words- Irish first:
Baille – house or home
Oiche- NIGHT , nightime or darkness
San oiche- at night
An areis – last night
Taibhse – ghost
Ceathair – cousin
Cailin – girl (colleen ?)
Pairc – field.
Teachin – cottage
Doras - door
Some notes:
Uncle Johnny calls his upper field 'the park' but it's just a
field not really like a park.
We say ' a wee doch an doras'.
Ask daddy what that means . Uncle johnnie didn't know.
Aunt Liza thinks it means a wee dram of whisky,
but I think she's only joking.

Diary : July 4th 1955

More new Irish words from uncle Johnnie, James and
Kathleen.

Bad iascaigh – fishing boat

Leorai –lorry

Sasta – glad

Mac – son

Ainm – name

TODAY'S NOTES

I can't say these words : iascaigh, ainm,leanbh.
Ask James.
We have a lot of Mac names in Glasgow, like the
MacPhersons who live next door
and the MacDonalds who live near the Roxy Picture House.
My best friend's name is Frank MacColgan and his
grannie came from a place near here called Carndonagh. He's
never been there.
*** Mammy's maiden name is McLaughlin.

I'm also learning this prayer that daddy likes
us to say. It's the Irish for the sign of the cross:

In ainm an Athar – In the name of the father
Agus an Mhic – and of the son
Agus an Spioraid Naoimh – and of the HOLY GHOST.
Amen

Chapter 3

Fishing on the Foyle

What a joy it was for a young Scot's boy to be out sailing
and fishing on the Foyle, with the hills of County Derry in the background.

Leaning excitedly on the half door of my Donegal cottage, I had often gazed down the wide sweep of fields to watch the fishermen out on the Foyle. Often, to get a better view, I would race through the uncut hay in the field in front of the house and leap over the hedge that guarded uncle Johnnie's lower field on the other side of the rodden.

There always seemed to be boats of all sizes out on the river ; punts, motor boats, coal boats and fishing trawlers ploughing busily through the waters. It was fascinating to watch them, all either heading out from the shoreline villages of Quigley's Point and Drung and Redcastle – out across the lough or down towards

Moville and out past Magilligan strand to the open waters of the North Channel.

The Foyle was like a magnet to us, always there glistening and swaying in the summer sun, or lit by moonlight, pulling its boats hither and thither as the tides rose and roared or lapped gently on the quiet accepting shores from Whitecastle down to Moville and up to Derry. My mother was always warning us about the Foyle, about its dangers and its deceptive lure. She often told us about the many local people, most of them young like us, who had been drawn to their early death by bathing in it out of view of adult help. She was always reminding us of the many fishermen, old and young who had left the shore never to return alive.

But it only fascinated me more and as I raced to the rodden and stared up past Crehenan and Hancock's house and up towards Quigley's Point, I couldn't resist the invitation I had from Willie Harrigan to go out with him to see what it was like out on the Foyle, actually fishing and being part of its swell and its hypnotic beauty. Although I say invitation from Willie, it was more that I had pestered and tormented him relentlessly every time I went down to my Uncle Dan's House and saw the neat, new punts Willie had on the shore and in the boatyard beside the house.

Willie to me was exciting and imaginative and totally different to Uncle Johhnie and Uncle Dan and my aunt Bridget's brother James. They were always there, ready to give advice, take us with them to the fields or up the hill to bring in the turf. But Willie was all about new boats and new ideas and the sea. Often, I knew he must have been bored out of his mind at my incessant, childish questions about the size of his punt or how often did he go out on the Foyle or what happened if the sea got rough or how many fish did he usually catch. Willie however never once lost his patience and always in his quiet, knowledgeable voice, would try his best to explain what happened out on the Foyle and remind me that it was all about experience. He would regale me about the currents and the tide and how to steer the boat in rough waters or through gaps in the rocks that lay dangerously close to some of the shoreline.

On the day Willie told me that the only way to find out about the Foyle was to go out and be in the boat and watch the nets being thrown in, I had left the cottage with my mother's worried blessing and his promise to her that I would be back no later than five for my tea with the family as usual. She knew that I had done my work around the house and that Uncle Johhnie was quite happy to see me for once leaving him at his fields on his own - getting on un – harrased with weeding the small field he had below the rodden- the one he called *The Garden*.

I raced down the rodden, out onto the Ruskey Road and went flying past Kathleen and Philomena's house, throwing back a casual glance and hoping that my sister Bridget wouldn't see me and want to come. As I pased the bottom of Barr's field, I stopped breathless and gazed down towards Willie Harrigan's house. Straight ahead of me I saw the enticing Foyle in bright, mid-day sunlight - gleaming in all its glory.

Willie and his son were out in the street in front of their house when I swung round past Uncle Dan's new wee cottage. Dan and Francie were up in Derry and remembering the fright I got getting into their house the previous week, I sped past the closed, brown door and I didn't take any last, lingering looks to see if the broken window had been repaired or not.

I had nothing but fishing on my mind now. I leapt onto the running board of the truck with Willie, Francis and I think it was Paddy Joe Callaghan in the driving seat, his right elbow resting casually on the driver's window ledge, a kind of sympathetic, slightly amused smile on his face. Willie hauled himself up beside Paddy Joe and gave Francis a helping hand into the driver's cabin and called on me to jump up onto the back of the truck and get a good grip on the two bars at the back of the driver's cabin.

Willie was never a man to waste his time on long-winded greetings or trivial conversations. I liked that in him and in Uncle Johnnie, but only when work or action was on offer. It was different when Bridget and I were out going round the houses visiting. Then we craved the long stories, the jokes, the long-winded reminiscences of days gone by and local news.We never tired of spending hours in dialogues in which we hardly ever said anything, but sat back and listened in awe to the never ending recollections of the fascinating people in our new Inishowen haven.

But there were no conversations now, as Paddie Joe revved up the lorry and swung it hard left out onto the Ruskey Road and down to the main Moville road. As he swung round part Armstrong's and past the wee cottage which lay sheltered under the cliff on the upper side of the road, my eyes gazed eagerly ahead, out along the shoreline of the Foyle and up to the rapidly approaching bay at Quigley's Point. There, in the warm afternoon sun, I could see three of four anchored punts, bobbing invitingly on the rising tide.

I had only once been out on a boat or punt since my arrival that year and that was the day Torrance took me in his Uncle's new boat down to Moville to the regatta. That had been an adventure and a half, but I had only been with Torrance as a passenger. Today I was going out from the shore, not skirting it – out towards the channel - out into the very heart of the Foyle.

The only other times I had been in a rowing boat was back home on Easter Sunday when my brother Paddy had taken us down to Bingham's Boating Pond - near the world-famous Botanic Gardens in Glasgow's West End. My boating experiences that day were very subdued and timid and closely controlled by my older brother. He was in charge and we would get chances to row from one end of the pond to the other, probably only a ten minute row, weaving in and out of the other small boats bobbing and swerving back and forth across the calm, untroubled ripples that took us from one end of the pond to the other.

But this was to be very different. This was fishing business and the aim was not to get to the crowds on Moville green, but to get up to the bay at Quigley's Point and get out on the Foyle and show that I could take it and come home with a nice armful of Salmon as a surprise and achievement.

When Paddy Joe swerved down the dirt track that lead down to the shingle beach at Quigley's Point, I was out of the back of the truck in a flash. But Willie had already made his way into the shallow water's edge, proudly pointing to his new knee – high Wellingtons and urging me to jump on his back to get a lift out to the punt. The others had no need to be carried to the punt, but were already in a race to get there first and start drawing in the long anchor rope and swing the punt round to face its bow out towards the Co Derry shore.

Willie eased me gently into the stern of the punt and they scrambled aboard, Willie quickly taking sharp pulls at the cord that would start up the outboard engine and get us out quickly to the channel and the spots where he knew shoals of fish would most likely be feeding.

Within ten minutes we were out past the Whitecastle Light, the engine stopped and the nets thrown out behind us as we drifted downstream with the current. I had always thought and hoped, in my ignorance of what fishing was all about, that a few minutes would then pass and we would start hauling in the nets with fish leaping about in them. I had no idea that we would now have to sit back and wait what to me was an interminable time, before any action was taken to bring in the nets. We all sat back in our different parts of the punt, Willie quietly moving us to our spots to balance the boat, organising the oars and easing up the outboard motor so that it stuck out vertically from the stern of the punt. He then produced a flask of tea and passed round some buttered scones as we bobbed gently up and down on the Foyle.

Although the others didn't talk that much, mainly questions to Willie about the movements of the tide and how they were going to organise the night's fishing, I could sense that they realised this was a big experience for me. As I lay back in the punt with my scone and mug of tea, I could see the coastline along the Foyle on either side.

For once in my holidays, the County Derry Coast was closest for a while and we could see the Royal Air Force planes sweeping up out of Eglinton Air Base and out down the Foyle, making their practice machine guns runs down the river towards Magilligan. Just past Eglinton I could see the white puffs of smoke from the Derry to Belfast train as it made its slow, twisting journey along the coastline past Ballykelly and Coleraine and round underneath the dominating mountain outline of Binevenagh. Further down the river I could make out other punts, scattered out along the Foyle - little hazy, bobbing outlines in the high afternoon sun.

The time dragged on and on and as I got used to the swell and the rise and fall of the boat, I realised that the one great quality that these fishermen needed was patience. I hadn't thought for a minute that our fishing expedition would have been getting out to the channel, getting the nets out and then waiting until the current hopefully drove the shoals of fish into them. But that's what it was and it was a fantastic learning experience for me. It made me realise that when it came to the sea, the fisherman had to play it at its own game – a game of watching and judging and waiting until the time was right to haul in the catch.

And it was a sudden shout from Willie that woke us from our afternoon daze and got us pulling together on the wet and heavy nets. We hauled and pulled in time to Willie's experienced shouts and instructions and soon I saw the magnificent sight of live salmon flapping about on the deck of the punt. It was my job to loosen them from the nets and throw them into the back of the punt. We caught seventeen salmon that day, magnificent, silver – sided, sparkling fish. As Willie pulled on the ripcord to get the outboard going and we headed back towards Quigley's Point, I was both relieved to see the shore looming up nearer - and proud that I had for once in my life been out with real, successful fishermen on the lough I loved.

My pride was even greater when I saw the delight on my mother's face when she saw me coming running up the lane safe - and with a large salmon proudly held in my open arms. That relieved and proud smile was reward enough to make the whole day one of the most memorable in my memories of Lough Foyle - and the wonderful fisher folk who made their living from it by day and night.

Chapter 4

Michael's Mobile Shop

My aunt Liza knew exactly when Michael's van would arrive at the lane. She got on with a her baking and could relax while Bridget and I sat on the ditch listening for every sound of the mobile shop.

To us young Scots visitors to Inishowen in the 1950's, Michael's Mobile Shop was an Aladdin's cave of tantalising Irish sweets, baps and biscuits - and a thousand other enticing delights. Everything seemed to taste and smell sweeter – alluring, captivating and the centre of our Inishowen world once every week.

Each Tuesday, my sister Bridget and I waited patiently on the van. We perched ourselves on the top of the ditch at the foot of our Uncle Johnnie's lane, our eyes eagerly scanning down the Ruskey Toad towards our aunt Bridget's cottage – straining for any sight of the white top of the van or the swirl of dust which would signal its arrival.

We swung round with excitement at every distant noise - our ears straining to catch the first familiar sounds of Michael's engine. We listened in the silence of the hills for the grinding of tyres on the road or the slamming of a door. Every sound meant that Michael was getting closer and closer - and our young hearts beat faster with excitement and suspense.

We knew that Michael would always turn up, come rain or sun and we knew his route almost as well as he did. So, we sat on the ditch working out the exact minutes it would take until we saw the van swerve past the rodden and up towards uncle Johnnie's lane and the cottage I was born in.

Our young minds told us that once Michael swung his van off the Derry - Moville Road and juddered up the steep, short hill at the foot of the Ruskey Road, he was on his way! We calculated how long he would take as he made his regular stops at uncle Dan's, Willie Harrigans, Charlie Grant and then up the steep slope to Kathleen and Philomena Barr's house - and then round the sharp left turn at Yankee Bridget's.

Sometimes we could hear the gears crunching as Michael nursed his old van up the twisting, turning brae. But these rough engine noises were welcome sounds as it meant he was nearly there and would have the tales of Willie Harrigan's new punt or the birth of a kid goat at Grants. Most importantly to us, he would have found out whether or not we would be allowed to go down and play in the Barr's wide field - or help them and their father Charlie with the hay. As well as being our mobile food provider, Michael always brought us exciting news and stories that appealed to our young minds and added to the magic of our waiting and the eventual arrival of his van.

Looking back now, it always seemed to be sunny and warm as we waited for Michael's van. Yet our real memories tell us that we often had to shelter from wind and rain. Then we would shelter under the ancient Birch tree that guarded the entrance to the lane up to Johnnie's cottage - and the magical, idyllic life in our Inishowen home.

So we sat entranced and enchanted, our legs crossed, our feet dangling over the ditch, clutching our money and the note that our mother had given us for the messages she needed for that week.

Our shopping experiences amid those Donegal hills were all so different from back in Glasgow. There we had to run a gauntlet through the tenement back courts and the grim, grey buildings not long recovered from the bombings of the Second World War. We would race along Gairbraid Avenue and across the dangerous Maryhill Road to the Co-Op or Sloan's Dairy and the fruit shops and the queues - and the noisy, jostling crowds. But our city shops, despite their variety and size, paled into insignificance when we heard the approaching rattle of Michael's van.

We jumped up when we heard the familiar thump of the van skirting over the huge boulder at the edge of the rodden. As Michael regained control of his van and swerved up the road towards us, we were down on him like dervishes – money spilling from our pockets and our notes flying in the air, money and notes only rescued by a careful practised swipe of the hand.

Although only sixteen or so himself, Michael seemed much older to us, used as we were with adults in most shops back home in Glasgow. But he relished our onslaught and he would shout out his cheery welcome to us as we raced down the road towards him.

He then carefully drew his van in to the side of the road, and, in what seemed to us one swift, superman movement, he had stopped the van, leapt from the driver's door and sprung round to open the back doors. He would then catapult himself inside and bring down the flap that he used as a counter. As he stood there, arms folded, smiling and with his order pad in his hand, we knew the big moment had at last arrived !

Of course we weren't the only shoppers glad to see Michael's van. Our wily but loveable Aunt Liza, through years of experience, had quietly judged the exact arrival time of the van from the half - door of the cottage. She slipped out - without a sound or without disturbing hens or cattle - and glided silently along the hedge that ran in front of our cottage. She slipped in through the little cluster of trees on the cottage side of the lane and straight out the slap at the foot of the lane. She was then at the exact spot where Michael had drawn up and where the van's back door lay invitingly open.

Michael always moved to serve Liza first, knowing, despite his young years, that Liza and the other neighbours were the life blood of the shop. He knew well that when all the Scotchies had gone home to Glasgow or Greenock or Paisley or Port Glasgow, his local customers would need the shop all year round. Michael knew that they would need him when the roads and the hills were covered with snow - and the cold icy winds blew down from Crehenan hill.

As we stood awe struck at Liza's sudden appearance, she ushered us gently in behind her. She then quickly handed Michael her roughly written note, patted us on the head and made her way busily back up to her baking and never-ending tidying up. She knew that once he had served us, Michael would pack her goods in a cardboard box and race up the lane with them and collect his money.

But now that we were at the van, we thrust our mother's note into Michael's hand. Trying to outdo each other, we blurted out our own childish demands for penny caramels, mint humbugs, sherbet bonbons and the Wagon Wheels he didn't have in his van the last time. He smiled at our frantic jumping and shouting and dipped and dived amongst what seemed like hundreds of boxes and bags. He then appeared in a cloud of flour dust, like a magician, with a bumper selection of our requests in his busy hands.

Michael the magician was now at work and we stood hypnotised by the speed and stunning accuracy of his deft footwork and his lilting singing voice. At the same time as beguiling us with his stories and news - and stuffing our hands with a never ending supply of sweets - Michael swiftly filled up our mother's shopping bag. As we took our change and slipped it into our pocket, Michael would leap out of the back door and race up the lane with Liza's messages, his jet black hair flowing in the wind as we scrabbled back up onto the ditch to see him off.

As he jerked the van into gear and it lurched forward and up the road and away from the lane – up towards the schoolhouse and the crossroads to Quigley's Point and Drung, we could see Michael glancing back at us through his side window. We always caught a re-assuring and caring smile on his face, knowing that he had hidden extra sweets as a surprise somewhere in the bags that we would open excitedly back in the cottage.

Michael knew that our long wait for him had got the rewards it deserved and we knew that somehow we had added some childish pleasure to his relentless journeys through the hills. We all knew that come the next Tuesday we would be sitting there on the ditch about eleven O'clock - waiting to go through the same magical charade.

We all knew that we would be listening and watching for the white top of the van to appear round the corner of the road and swerve to avoid the boulder at the foot of the rodden. Then, when we saw the van in its full, battered glory, we knew we would experience once again our never to be forgotten shopping moments in the hills of Inishowen.

Diary : July 14th
More Irish Words

I'm learning more and more Irish words for daddy coming over. Last night a friend of Aunt Ellen's from America came in late at night. Willie Joe was his name. Uncle Johnnie said he could stay the night. They let him sleep in the Settle Bed and I slept down in the room. He told us stories about places called Culdaff and Malin. He was from a place called Gleneely. He spoke IRISH and gave me the Irish words for places to look out for around Ruskey.

Loch Feabhail means Loch Foyle. They say Caislean Ban for Whitecastle, Caislean Dearg for Redcastle and Caistle an Nua for Greencastle.

That means ban is white, dearg is red and nua is green.

Quigley's Point up the road is a difficult one to say. It is Rinn Mhic Choigligh in Irish. We just say we're going up to Carrowkeel.

Going down the lower road the other way, the other places you come to are Drung, Clar and then Moville.

I couldn't get the Irish for Drung, but somebody said it might be Drong.

Clar is the same in Irish, just CLAR.

Moville has two names in Irish. The first one is Magh Bille and the another one is Bun an Phoiball.

Another big town is Carndonagh, which is almost the same in irish, CARNDOMNAGH.

The main town we all know is Derry – NOT Londonderry. The Irish for Derry is DOIRE. St Columba came from there to Scotland.

Chapter 5

Animal Magic

' To us young Scots from the city, an everyday chore like feeding the hens was a magical experience'

Coming from busy city streets in Glasgow, where the only animals we ever saw regularly were a stray dog or cat, we were all amazed at how animals of all kinds were so much part of everyday life in our Donegal cottage and in the world around Ruskey. Back in Scotland, our only real experiences with animals was when we were taken to the Calderpark Zoo or on one special occasion by the school as far as Edinburgh Zoo. But it was always a kind of artificial although enjoyable connection to the animal world. Having to be taken to see animals at a distance, made us detached from them as if they were part of another world.

So when we returned to our streets around Maryhill, we felt lucky if the odd cart and horse was spotted now and again, either the 'rag –man' blowing his bugle and leading his scraggy disinterested pony, or the briquettes seller, his horse covered from head to toe in coal dust and desperate to get his load hauled along and out to graze down at the grasses alongside the nearby river Kelvin.

From the first day we arrived at our Donegal cottage, however, animals were everywhere around us – both outside and inside the house. Aunt Liza was crazy about Collie dogs and I can't remember a summer when there weren't one or two around the Ruskey cottage - a new one quickly replacing her loss when the old ones died or occasionally were killed.

Aunt Liza had a devoted and at the same time confrontational relationship with her Collies, mostly called Prince or Jewel. To her they were a devoted part of her family and were tenderly cared for through the long winter nights when other less fortunate dogs had to wander and roam the Inishowen byways to get enough to survive on or shelter in an old unlocked barn. In return, Aunt Liza's Collies were fanatically protective of her and saw her as 'the master' even to the exclusion of Uncle Johnnie. Although they would come to his call or bidding around the house or out herding cattle, you could almost feel that if Aunt Liza wasn't there, they were responding reluctantly, more out of respect for Aunt Liza rather than genuine obedience to uncle Johnnie.

But if she was around, they would stick to her like glue, snaking around her apron as she swished in and out of the half – door on her hundred and one duties ; hanging out washing, going for water to the well, feeding the chickens and hens and the odd duck and goose she had managed to buy. As she diligently swept up and washed around the slabs at the entrance to the cottage, they would slither and slide as she threw buckets of water across the scrubbed surface and repositioned her beloved geranium pots on either side of the cottage door.

I don't ever remember Aunt Liza ever raising her voice or shouting at them to obey her commands. She always seemed to be able to get their complete attention and control by simply glancing at them or pretending she was moving to get the kitchen brush or flicking her apron out in mock anger. It was as if they could read her moods and commands even as she was thinking them, and that Liza and her dogs were on a wave-length that was their own and into which we couldn't connect.

For at the same time, all her Collie's were jealous when we came, as if somehow they sensed that we were strangers, visitors who had come from afar and wouldn't be there to feed and look after them when the November storms and winter frosts clutched their cottage and fields in its bitter grip.

I remember especially Prince that summer of 1955, a black and white abandoned waif of a dog that Aunt Liza had saved from a bag of pups thrown into the river to drown. Prince was indeed a royal inhabitant in our lovely Donegal cottage and he knew it. He knew that in Aunt Liza's eyes he could do no wrong and in return, he would always be totally and utterly loyal and reliable. Prince never actually made any direct move towards us, to threaten us. But his reluctance to make us feel at ease was more disconcerting than any direct barking or scowling, knowing as he did that Aunt Liza would be angry and he would be somehow letting her down – something that he was totally incapable of.

To show us his regal position in the cottage and his knowledge that Aunt Liza reigned supreme, he would edge over towards us and sneak underneath our seats as we sat at the table or at the fire. The look on his eyes was never threatening, but neither was it comforting or welcoming! It was as if he was letting us know that he would tolerate our human company in his beloved Liza's presence – but that was it. He never responded in any playful way to our patting him, but stood or lay obediently, glancing up at Aunt Liza with sad, appealing eyes. I think he mostly hoped that he would be even more in her favour if he patronised the noisy, alien, harsh Scots - tongued children who had suddenly disrupted the peace and quiet of his cottage life.

But then Collies weren't Aunt Liza's only animal friends and she showered her affection with abundance in words and actions on her cows, calves, hens and geese. To her, the animals – all of them - were individuals in their own right and weren't simply there to provide a sale at the Carndonagh market or eggs for the breakfast or milk for the churn. She knew of course, like all her neighbours, that her animals provided them with the basics of everyday life of meat and eggs and milk – but she never saw them or ever treated them as just that.

That glorious first year, Aunt Liza had two cows and a calf and was devotedly proud of them and treated them with great affection – even in the most mundane and simplistic of tasks – like feeding hay or water to them or coaxing milk out of her favourite cow Nellie.

Aunt Liza swore she had never had such a docile, valuable cow as Nellie and would caress and talk to her gently as she either urged her out of the byre in the early dawn or cajoled her to come into the byre for milking in the late evening. I was always astounded at the simple, yet noble sight of Aunt Liza milking Nellie. When the time came to bring her and her calf down from the upper park and along to the crossroads and down to the barn, Liza would go into a kind of performance. She would take us aside and talk to us and warn us of the importance of being careful and not using our sticks unless there was danger or if Nellie was in any way becoming awkward. Aunt Liza always pointed out of course that any disobedience on Nellie's part would be because we strangers to her and not able to whisper or sing the comforting words and sounds that her favourite cow was used to.

We were only given the odd opportunity (and to Aunt Liza – the privilege) to take one of Uncle Johnnie's walking sticks and go up to the park and bring Nellie home. To Liza, it was a brief break from a daily duty and allowed her to catch up on some other chore ready for Nellie coming down to be milked. To us, it was a momentous, onerous task and one we embarked on with determination and pride- and at times great sense of fear in case anything should go wrong.

We need never have feared !

As we raced up towards the crossroads on our mission, we glanced back every now and again to catch a glimpse of Aunt Liza's alert yet uneasy figure on the huge rock behind the cottage, hand over her eyes to shield them from the dipping sun. From the elevated huge boulder, Aunt Liza could keep a close eye on our movements, then dart back to the cottage to whip a scone out of the oven and then appear again - so that at no stage in the journey were we totally out of her sight.

Although in those days there was little danger from busy, racing cars or speeding lorries in the quiet roads leading up to the field

Uncle Johnnie lovingly called *the park* and back home, aunt Liza was never totally at ease at passing over the safety of her little herd of two to unreliable though well - intentioned Scottish herders. She nipped rapidly in and out of the cottage from the moment we left until her animals were safely coming up the lane and round the front of the cottage.

As Nellie and her docile calf passed the front door, aunt Liza would unhinge her apron, throw it onto the top of the half-door and rush to swing open the half -rotted door of the cattle shed. Only then, when Nellie and her calf were safely in and the door bolted, would aunt Liza give us a pat on the back or a word of praise. She would thankfully usher us into the kitchen and cut us both a large slice of the scone she had just baked and smother it with our favourite Irish butter. As we sat back at the side of the turf fire and aunt Liza majestically whipped up the bucket to go and milk Nellie, we realised that we had experienced just a few precious moments in the world of aunt Liza's small but magical animal kingdom.

Diary : July 19 th: Words for Daddy

Daddy will be here tomorrow and I've now learned more words and another prayer as I promised him I would try my best. I've found some Irish words that are nearly the same as ours. It was easier to remember them as they sounded much the same. Here they are.

Mathair, mother	Litir, letter	**The words I found very strange are:**
Athair, father	Cuirtin, curtain	
Scoil, school	Vasa, vase	
Cat, cat	Lampa, lamp	Builin, bread
Plata, plate	Veain, van	Ubh, egg
Forc, fork	Bus, bus	Subh, jam
Cupan, cup	Clog, clock	Uisce, water
Leitis, lettuce	Stol, stool	Cearc, hen
Geata, gate		Muc, pig
Bagun, bacon		Bo, cow
Baisin, basin		

Special Diary Notes:

I'm trying to learn the OUR FATHER in Irish as I know daddy will be very pleased if I can say it to him. I got the first part from Dr McGurk down at St Columba's in Drung after Mass on Sunday. I'll try and get the other words from Daddy or maybe Master Smith.

Ar nAthatai, ata ar neamh	Our Father who art in heaven
Go naofar d'ainm	Hallowed be thy name.
Go taga do ríocht	Thy kingdom come
Go deantar do thoil ar an talamh	Thy will be done on earth,
Mar a deantar ar neamh	As it is in heaven.

Here are some of the words from the next line, but I don't know 'us' or 'our'

Give, tabhair,
This day, Today, inniu
Daily, laethuil
Bread, aran

Chapter 6

Dancing Lights over Drung

My sister Bridget plans to go and see the dancing lights over Drung. Her cousins Patricia and Maureen can't wait to hear what happens

A crimson sun dipped down behind Crehenan Hill as my sister Bridget and I slipped quietly out of our uncle Johnnie's Donegal cottage. Our dad was now over from Glasgow and my brother Martin had gone back to his job. That night our mum and dad were going down to Dan and Francie's house for their dinner. So it was a big night for uncle Johnnie and aunt Liza to be going out for their dinner, as they usually provided the food and had all the visitors in their house.

But, unknown to anyone in the house other than our brother John, we were setting out on our first mysterious and enchanting night journey to meet our cousins Katie and Sadie. Our older brother John, always protective but knowing where we were going that night, had teased us the night before as we lay on the huge straw mattress beds in the lower room. We knew that he was making it all so much more scary and dangerous, but in a way it made us all the more determined to meet our two older cousins and take up the 'dare' of going to see the dancing lights.

These two night guides would take us on our first ever journey to see the mysterious, scary, dancing lights in the high fields on the upper road to Drung - the nearest town to our summer Ruskey home. We glided silently down the cobbled lane behind the old thatched cottage, never daring for a second to look back or slow down in case our mother or our Aunt Liza would hear us - and end our mystery night journey even before it had even begun.

Aunt Liza, always warm and comforting yet at times devilishly scary, knew how easily we were snared into the country tales about Inishowen ghosts and goblins. She had often teased us as night drew in around the turf fire and the Summer sky darkened about the dangers of dabbling in what she called the 'other world and the wee folk '.

We always knew – or at least hoped - that our Aunt Liza was teasing - just teasing us. We knew she would have that little, devilish glint in her eyes and would pause every now and again in her stories just to glance behind us or go suddenly to the hearth door as if to just make sure that there was nobody there and nothing to be afraid of. Like so many of those wonderful Donegal wives and mothers, she was an actress in the grand manner in her small, insignificant but enchanting Inishowen cottage.

Although we were actually scared out of our wits sometimes, she often kept us enthralled and bewitched talking by the flickering light of a Tillie lamp well into the midnight hours. We gasped as she told us about the rider - less white horse from Cabry which could be seen on windy, moonlit nights galloping over the upper road. She whispered silently as she told us how the horse galloped wildly in a desperate, eerie never ending search for the young lover he had thrown from his saddle to his death on the night before his wedding.

But we were outside now and the warmth and glow of the turf fire was behind us and we were being drawn down the lane and out onto the road where we would be able to make out our two guides – our cousins Katie and Sadie.

As we nervously turned right at the bottom of the lane and edged our way up the Ruskey Road towards the schoolhouse, we could just make out the two shadowy figures coming smartly down the road towards us.

Katie and Sadie were inseparable and had looked after us like big sisters since we arrived on that first idyllic return to our homeland above the Foyle. Nothing seemed a bother to them and they walked for miles to take us to Drung to church for our first mass - and into houses to talk and sing in the evenings. We had only to ask and they would go out of their way to take us to meet other distant cousins and the older generation of relations who had grown up with our mother.

Everybody knew Katie and Sadie and yet as people they were totally different. Katie, dark and sallow with long flowing black hair, was always in command of any situation. She was the one who did the introductions and made us all feel at home wherever we went on our visits and out on our childish expeditions over *Cundum* and *Upper Drung* and as far down as *The Red Brae* or even *Redcastle*.

Sadie

~~Katie~~ was smaller, with light brown hair and more at ease taking a back seat when Katie was around. She trusted her sister implicitly and was totally happy to be there with her, whether it was looking after the family up in Drung or in the shops, or looking after her two young cousins from Scotland who saw all of these experiences as marvellous and exciting.

So, in the engulfing darkness we ran suddenly towards them and clasped their hands, Bridget on the inside of the road, with Katie and Sadie in the middle and me holding tightly onto Sadie's soft hand on the outside. For a few moments I felt that I was their guardian - their protector, the knight on the outside, right hand ready and free to draw the sword if any threat came to put us in danger or peril.

But my boldness vanished swiftly as we moved forward and into the darkness and round the corner of the schoolhouse and along the upper Ruskey Road. On our right, we could just hear the soft,eerie rustle of the wind in the moss and among the dark rushes on the right side of the road. As our soft footsteps echoed silently on the sandy road, we clasped our hands together tighter and moved towards the fields higher up on the side of the hill –

high up above Mannie's house where we could just make out a faint light, half hidden in the darkness by a curtain and the high hedge in front of the house.

As we passed our Uncle Johnnie's field on the left side, a brief, unsettling shudder ran through my veins as I thought I caught a glimpse of a shadowy figure slipping in behind the ditch, just beyond the gate into the field. I had often wondered why our uncle Johnnie had called this field The Secret Park and never encouraged us to come up to it when the hay was being cut or a fence repaired or tea was being brought up for the midday break. He always seemed more willing to welcome us when we went down to the fields in front of the house and across the rodden, the ones behind James's house or the ones lower down on the edge of the Ruskey Road.

But as we passed the Park field and the momentary shudder of fear left me, we drew closer and closer together, as if we were becoming one being – watching, listening, hearing and fearing all in one. It was the total silence now that frightened me most and began to instil the first feelings of wishing that we had never ventured out, or had left coming out until when it wasn't so dark or until we were in a bigger group with our parents and brothers.

But we were there now in the midst of the silence and the fields and the trembling hands. It had all come so suddenly the feeling of fear. One minute we were in awe, chatting with Katie and Sadie and listening so quietly to them talking to us about all the times they had gone out at night and seen the lights - and come back and talked about it to their own family and friends.

But that meant nothing now as they too suddenly became silent and slowed their pace and began to point uneasily up towards the three dark trees on our left just beyond uncle Johnnie's beloved field. We stopped dead and stood staring into the darkness, never daring to move an inch and waiting transfixed to catch any glimpse of any kind of light or brightness in that Inishowen darkness.

And then we saw them, dancing and flickering along the top edge of the field and moving down toward us and then moving back as if into their own hiding places. The lights shone brightly and then faded and then shone even brighter still - as we clutched each other and the sweat broke out on our brows.

I can remember vividly the feeling of adolescent fear out there in the dark and silence of the upper Ruskey Road. But then my sense of realism and boyish bravado and desire to appear braver than I was took over. As we all stood motionless and to the complete amazement of my sister Bridget and Katie and Sadie, I let out the most awful, loud, and sudden Tarzan like yell that echoed up through the fields and up along the side of the high hedge where the lights were dancing..

As the sudden echoing yell sound broke the silent, still air, the lights along the hedge went out in a complete instance. I could feel the others turning towards me and then Katie and Sadie ushering my sister and I back along the road towards the schoolhouse and past my Uncle Johnnie's field.

With quickened steps we moved more easily and with some short, whispered words about what we had seen and how we had done the right thing on our holidays and how we would be sure to tell all our pals about seeing the lights the minute we were back in Scotland.

As we turned down the Ruskey Road towards our cottage and neared the break in the school hedge that led into the well where we collected our daily water, our Uncle Johnnie strode out, a bucket in each hand. We gazed at him for a few seconds in disbelief - and then in sheer relief that he was on the road and would walk us all back down the rest of the way and up the lane into the cottage.

As we strolled contented along behind him in the soft glow of the rising moon, I noticed that his old battered, torch swung wildly from his belt. I said nothing to the others and they strolled on down towards the lane - totally engrossed in their reminiscences of having seen the lights dancing high above the hedge up on the upper road to Drung.

Diary : Sunday 31 st July

What a day!

Met my secret Irish sweetheart for the first time.

Met her at mass in Drung at St Columba's.

Mammy said I was baptised there during the war.

Secret Poem:

I think I'll write this poem I learned at school on a sheet of paper and send it secretly to her. It's by my favourite poet at school called Robert Burns. I've changed the words a wee bit for her.

Oh my luv is like a red, red rose
that's newly sprung in June.
Oh my luv is like a melody
that's sweetly played in tune.
So fair thou art ma bonnie lass,
so deep in luv am I.
And I will luv ye still my dear
till aw the seas gang dry.
Till aw the seas gang dry
my dear
an' the rocks melt wae the sun.
An' I will luv ye still my dear
till the sands o' time shall run.

I'll put 'from a secret admirer'.

I hope my Inishowen Beauty likes my poem and the flower I've taken for her from aunt Liza's garden.

Chapter 7

First Kiss

One of the loveliest and most enduring memories I have of my Inishowen holidays was making new friends with other young people my own age and finding out about love for the first time.

When I look back now, both the innocence and the intensity of those new feelings astounds me and I can still feel the magic of that summer love. But our parents knew - and the parents of the friends we met knew - that holiday romances and escapades and dares would always be near the surface as we mixed with boys and girls and played talked and learned about growing up.

As we moved out from the shelter of our Donegal cottage, from visiting the older people and listening to their tales and stories, we started to meet more and more young people of our own age. First of all it was through working out in the fields with our uncle Johnnie and Aunt Liza and then bringing in the turf for neighbours or running errands to Maggie's shop at the brow of the Ruskey Road.

I remember we loved the way our new young friends talked – their Irish accent - so different from our harsher Scots tongue- made even more foreign to our friends by the Glasgow slang we spoke. But our friendships and the games we played and the excitement of our times together in the fields and roads of Inishowen gave us a universal language - and kept us together and gave us a new bond that we never thought existed.

And yet it wasn't in the middle of our games or adventures or work in the fields that I found my first stirrings of those beautiful youthful feelings of love for an Irish girl. This great event in my Donegal holidays came in St Columba's Church in Drung during Mass.

To us young visitors from Scotland, going down to Mass on a Sunday in Donegal seemed a more enriching and more dramatic experience than anything back in Glasgow. As the week drew to a close we could feel that everything seemed to be building up to something special and that clothes had to be got ready and shoes cleaned and hair washed and tidied.

We were also amazed that we had a long journey to make as opposed to the short journey back home in Maryhill in Glasgow. There, we only had to leave fifteen minutes before Mass started, rush up Stirrat Street, over the canal and along the short stretch of Maryhill Road to get to our local church - The Immaculate Conception.

But in Inishowen, we loved the whole preparation and importance of getting ready for Mass. We loved the idea that to go to Mass we would have to go to another town, not just along the road for a ten minute walk. The very fact that we had to leave an hour before Mass gave the whole day and its preparations and its journey a greater kind of spiritual importance to us. All of these things added to the importance of this event in the lives of the people we loved - and more so in our own, as we tried to fit into and understand the new world we were in - high up in the countryside above The Foyle.

Faithfully, every Saturday night, my sister Bridget and I would get our best clothes cleaned and ironed and under the gentle but firm gaze of our mother, tidy them away neatly on hangers in the lower room

On most journeys to Mass, we had no car or bus to take us there and we strode off as a family on the stroke of 10.O'clock to walk along the rodden, down the lower Ruskey road and out on to the main Derry - Moville Road towards Drung.

I can remember so well those silent, almost sanctified journeys, Bridget, John and myself shining like new pins. As we skirted the fields and trod the Donegal roads, we walked with care to make sure that no puddles or dust tarnished our appearance. We were so proud as we journeyed together down to Mass. Somehow, we loved the whole feeling of seeing the church high up on the hill as we got nearer Drung and then coming up the church brae and into the church with the organ music drifting out to meet us.

The music and singing from the back of the church always enthralled me at St Columba's in Drung. I remembered writing a school essay about it back at St Mungo's Academy in Glasgow, trying with great joy to describe the wonderful experience I had felt and how different it had all seemed from city masses back home in the in Glasgow.

The Mass was flowing beautifully that morning I first felt those first sweet and tender feelings. At the Communion Hymn my sister and I quietly stood up to move along the row towards the centre to go down to Communion. For some unknown reason, I stumbled slightly over someone's foot and as I turned embarrassed to get my bearing I gazed over at the choir.

It was then at that moment that I first caught a glimpse of her, the first girl in my life to rouse the most amazing and beautiful feelings of love which was totally different from anything I had ever experienced before.

After those feelings and building up the courage to ask her out – to 'go with me' as we said in Glasgow – whatever that meant, We went out together as often as WE could – often in secret meetings along the river, down by the shore, in our own special places. During all that time of feeling special to each other and secret walks and special plans and jokes and stories - I faltered to make the special move to kiss to seal our special feelings.

But then, one regatta evening after we had all returned back from the sailing and the shows and the music in Moville, we sneaked quietly down the lane to the shore that led out to the little bay. The Foyle glistened in the soft moonlight that summer evening and I can vividly remember the waves lapping on the shore on the beach. Looking back now, of course, I can rationalise it all and put it down to childish infatuation or holiday emotion, but no - one has ever since then been able to explain why that spark should suddenly come at that moment in time, in that place and for that one particular girl.

Just my secret Inishowen sweetheart and I. Just the two of us – both Irish but from totally different worlds - drawn to each other we knew not why. But it was joyful and exciting and totally overwhelming. With her, Everything seemed soft and dreamy as if it we were in a wonderful new world with the best of everything and the sounds of the waves lapping up on the shore.

I look back now and wonder often. Did it happen really happen or did I imagine it all? Why should this one moment stick so vividly in my mind? And then I can recall again and again the soft sand on my shoulders and can see the fishing boats at the edge of the bay, with The Foyle in the background.

And her sweet lips and soft, words. And yet it was all so innocent and tender - silences and being overwhelmed by the stunning intensity of it all. It was as if we were the only two people in the world at that time,

And yes we were so young and so simple in our emotions that we both knew that this was something totally new and beautiful and overpowering. I never at any time felt that there was anything wrong in our kiss and the secrets we shared and the great plans we had for meeting when we were older – wherever we might live. We both felt naively at such a young age that our world was now settled and that somehow we would always be like this and our beautiful love would go on forever.

But as always in these glorious, but often brutal years of our youth, the magic of those moments at Drung along the shore, as the Foyle glistened in the background, all came to a halt as we went our separate ways – my Inishowen sweetheart back to her life in Drung and I back to the harsh realities of city life!

As the promised letters died out and the winters came in and the tender promises were lost in the months of separation, the great plans for the future died out in the torrent of adolescence back in

Scotland. But the beauty, the sweetness and the never-ending meaning of that first kiss will live with me forever.

Diary: August 4th

OUR SONG ?

I heard this song on Fiorentini's juke box in Moville and I thought about my secret love. It's a song by Pat Boone and it's in the charts. I didn't see her last week as she was at her cousin's place. The song is called ' Love letters in The Sand' and it reminds me of being down at Drung shore with her.

'On a day like today, we passed the time away,
Writing love letters in the sand.
How you laughed when I cried, each time I saw the tide,
Wash our love letters from the sand.'

An Irish Poem:

I'm going to write some words of my own
in irish for her and sign it .
It might impress her. I could post it to her house.
I hope I got most of the words ok.

Gra is fior – love is true.
Gra is alain– love is beautiful.
She is alain – She is beautiful.

Le gra o Stephen xxxx

Note on My Diary Entry from 1955

When I look back at my childish attempts to ' show off' to My inishowen sweetheart by trying to write to her in Irish, I still get a warm, happy feeling that at least I tried. I am still proud that the people around me then tried to help and encourage my faltering, attempts at trying to deal with new , strong feelings for my Irish sweetheart.

If I could only have had real knowledge of the Irish then, what I would have given to write out the poem correctly. But looking back now, and thinking of the innocence and magic of that lovely summer evening on the shore, I know that she was pleased that I had made the effort for her. I never remember her even trying to correct what I had written down in the poem and I'm sure she could easily have done so.

If only I could have written it like this!

Is fíor an gra.
Is alainn an gra
Ta tu alainn
Ta me i ngra leat.

Le gra o Stephen

How magical it would have been if I could have put down the few words I knew of the Pat Boone song into Irish. How I would have been over the moon to see her face light up with pride.

Love letters in The Sand

Ar la mar an la seo,
Chuir muid thart an t –am.
Ag scríobh litreacha gra sa ghainim

Chapter 8

The Forbidden Bike

My brother Paddy wisely guards uncle Johnnie's bike. Paddy brought his own racer over from Scotland and won at the Quigley's Point Sports

It never once occurred to me until I was older how much my Uncle Johnnie treasured his bike. To him, the bike was an invaluable friend and trusted companion who should never be touched or used willy nilly just to race up and down the Ruskey Road.

To Bridget and I from the streets of Glasgow, a bike was something for young people to race at breakneck speed around the streets and lanes of our Maryhill tenements. We were bamboozled by the very idea that somebody could put so much importance on and give so much care and attention to a cold, mechanical frame.

Back home in Glasgow, our brother Paddy had a new racing bike and most of our friends had bikes. Any chance we got after school or at weekends, we whizzed and zoomed with them as gangs – and loaned them out and shared them as we raced and scrambled around the streets from morning till night – pretending we were daredevils.

To Uncle Johnnie however, his bike was sacred. He kept it lovingly under lock and key in the tidiest and most protected part of the outhouse nearest the front door. As he passed to and fro across the front of the house, he would gaze in affectionately and often double check the lock to make sure that no Scotchy children's fingers had been tampering at it. In dry weather, when the dust cascaded up from the dry roads, he caressed it with oil and water as if he was almost blessing it in a sacred kind of ceremony or ritual he had learned as a boy.

When he went out on the bike it was another ritual that I had never seen in my life and would never cease to wonder at. He would swiftly unlock the bike and hide the key in some nook or cranny in the outhouse, knowing that we would never find it. He would then wheel the bike reverently out and round the small whitewall that ran across the driveway in front of the cottage. He would then lean it softly against the bush that grew at the end of the wall, slip on his bicycle clips, gently mount his bike and glide swiftly past the cottage and down the lane. There was never any rush or jerking or bumping and I could never be anything but inspired that something so basic could be given so much care and be of such importance in someone's everyday life.

In answer to our astonished questions at why Uncle Johnnie had such reverence for the bike - and why he never bumped it roughly over the cobbled stones in front of the cottage, my mother let us know how precious he saw his bike. She reminded us that she had only on one occasion know that he had bundled the bike across the cobbled stones and raced roughly and swiftly down the lane. It had been on that balmy September afternoon when she had felt the first stirrings of myself in her womb.

She had not been well throughout this pregnancy she said and had wanted the doctor to be there in case wee Mary wasn't able to get to be at my birth.

Uncle Johnnie on that eventful day had rushed to the bike and broken all his rituals and was on the Ruskey Road in seconds, racing pell -mell down past the Barr's house, down the steep hill and headlong towards the lower road. The nearest doctor was in Drung, four miles away and Uncle Johnnie never stopped for a breath until he was skidding to a halt in front of the doctor's front window. To his sheer delight, the doctor was in and rushed up in his car to the Ruskey cottage in time - twenty minutes before I started to come into my Inishowen world.

Uncle Johnnie was never one to hurry or lose his temper or rush to get started on any of the thousand farmyard tasks he did day in day out. He worked as he talked - slowly, with thought and attention given to the most ordinary questions we asked him about the size of chickens or how high hay grew or where cattle slept if they were out in the field all night.

During the glorious, never ending days in our Donegal hills, we had a million innocent, baffling and at times utterly pointless questions which to Uncle Johnnie and our other relatives, friends and neighbours must have seemed despairing. But to us it was all so new and exciting and important. Even the most ordinary, simple incidents, tales and events of daily life had a magic and a mystery which was at times overpowering and always fascinating.

What we eventually began to realise as the summer days passed, was that the bike was in no way magical or mysterious to Uncle Johnnie. To him it was his most valuable possession outwith the actual cottage and the essential furniture, clothes and dishes inside.

In rain or sun, his bike was always there, neatly cleaned and checked ready for use every day and night. Whether it was to take him up to his beloved Park Field to painstakingly pick the weeds from rows of lettuces or to chase after some wayward, fugitive cow, Uncle Johnnie knew that his bike was there - and he protected it with pride.

To us, however, the bike was simply a toy, something that you could get on to and whirl down the lane, along past the rodden and swerve to a dramatic stop outside our Aunt Bridget's at the top of the Ruskey Road. But because of its forbidden status, Uncle Johnnie's bike seemed more enticing and inviting to us because of the protection he gave it and the secret methods he took to guard it. Without ever actually telling us that we couldn't use it to play on, he made sure in his own subtle, quiet but absolutely no nonsense way that no youngsters leapt on it with abandon or put it through swerves and races and skids on the dusty summer Donegal roads.

As the summer days went in and we gave up our childish, but totally pointless begging to get a wee shot on the bike, we gave in and accepted the unpalatable fact that he wouldn't change his mind or waver from his quiet stance. We therefore sought out bikes of all kinds anywhere else we could, down at Barrs or along at our upper road relatives in Mannie's where Johnnie could always be won over by our persistant, childish pleadings. He would smilingly allow us to take shots on his bike - from his house along the upper road to the Crossroads and back.

Often as we passed by Uncle Johnnie at the hay or mending fences around his upper field – the park, he would wave down benignly to us and watch with polite interest as we wobbled and swayed our way back and forth along the upper road a thousand times. But never once did he ever show any annoyance that we had gone elsewhere to get a ride on a bike, or that anyone might wonder why he wouldn't allow us to go any further than the short distance between the cottage lane and the well below the school.

We just accepted the quiet, respect he gave to his bike and felt privileged if he allowed us to occasionally bring it out of the shed to clean it or mend a puncture. And if he crowned our efforts with a chance to ride it in front of him up to the well and back - then we were really in cycling heaven !

Chapter 9

Music over Moville

Music echoes over Moville on regatta day. A boat race is about to start. The crowds are on the green.
Stephen and his Ruskey friends are on the diving board at the bathing boxes - waiting for the swimming race

In those golden summer days in Inishowen, the two towns most imprinted on my mind were Derry and Moville.

My memories of Derry in those days are of The Lairds Loch, the waterfront and our first glorious footsteps on Irish soil on our way back home to Inishowen. I remember Derry mostly at dawn as her streets lay silent and only the quayside bustled into life as we all made our ways to the buses and taxis and coaches that would take us to the cottages and people we loved.

Derry was a kind of mystical, momentary city - only glimpsed in haste as we all threaded our way through the empty streets. It was only in later life that Derry became a real, living tortured city. Little did we all know then that the same quiet, tantalising streets would echo around the world with tragedy and tears and torment. But that was to be in another time, as yet unknown to us in our childish summer fantasy world.

The real centre of our Inishowen world, and the town to which we were drawn, was Moville. I first heard the name Moville during my Whitecastle holidays in the strangest of places. It was when I was helping Charlie Barr bring in the turf from high up on Glencaw Hill. The boys I was with then, Billie and Albert Doherty, Hugh Hancock and the Davenports were new and exciting friends – full of fun and mystery and devilment. As we helped with the turf, we jostled and played and talked after our long day in the summer sun high above the distant shores of the Foyle. To me this was a totally new enchanting world. It was a world of stories and tales of the old people who had brought home the turf on their own back - or if they were lucky on the back of a donkey. They had maybe made twenty journeys to the hill as the summer sun sunk low earlier each day to herald the beginning of Autumn.

Our journey back down through Glencaw and over the Mullinroe Bridge was full of singing and laughter and, as we clung onto the ropes that held in the turf and kept us from flying off onto the road, the constant talk came up about Moville and sailing and a regatta.

Although Glasgow was my where I lived and I was near the river Clyde and boats and ships that made their way across the seven seas, I had never heard of nor been to a regatta. To us that was for the ' toffs ' : doctors and lawyers and business people who went at weekends down to Clydeside resorts such as Helensburgh or Troon to sail their yachts for prestige and to relax in luxury among the Scottish isles from their weekly business duties and routines.

I loved the sound of the word Moville and wondered where it was and how you got to it and what new adventures and mysteries it held for us. Aunt Liza had told us about 'the far town' which to our amazement was less than half a mile away across the rodden in front of our cottage. We were amazed to find that this 'far town' had only two or three houses and was no further than a five minute walk. This was where Old Jane lived and the Davenports and Wee Mary - the marvellous, wise wee lady who had brought me into the world in our dimly lit Ruskey cottage during the harvest - on the fifteenth of September 1941.

But to our city minds, Edinburgh or Aberdeen or London would be classed as far towns, but in the idyllic wonderland of the Inishowen hills, the actual nearness of the far town of Lower Ruskey gave us some indication about the smallness of the world we were now living in. We now knew that we were cut off from the real world of distances and miles and concrete streets and roads and tram car lines and tall buildings.

But where was Moville ?

And why was there such interest in it high up on the hills as we stuggled to fill the hired lorry and pack its sides to the brim and get finished and get home to tea and scones and bed. It was the regatta they were talking about. They were saying that it would soon be taking place - now that August was coming in and the hay was being cut and stacked in the fields along the Foyle and the carts were bringing loads of turf down the twisting, winding rough tracks.

But Billy said he had heard that this year was going to be the best ever for the Whitecastle sailing team. His dad and uncles and cousins had a new punt – a special Whitecastle punt, kept closely guarded and tested in the evenings around the shore at Whitecastle House. I was overawed that he talked of a castle and secret sailings - and trophies. And I couldn't wait until I could find out more from my Uncle Johnnie and Aunt Liza as we sat around the turf fire that evening after the exhausting day on Crehenan Hill.

Uncle Johnnie had only been once to the regatta but what he told me about its magic and the people and the atmosphere meant that I would have to go. I remember my mother telling me that her father would often walk the two hour journey to Moville from Ruskey, through Redcastle, down past Clar and out round the old pier and into the town.

But walking like that was nothing to my grandparents. The walk to Moville was nothing to the dawn walk he would make every June - the whole way to Derry - to uncomplainingly work his fare on the Lairds Loch and go to Scotland to earn a few extra pounds to send home to Ruskey. It was strange - and baffling to us that our grandfather had to travel to Scotland to earn some money as a seaman on the pleasure boat The Iona. We couldn't seem to understand why he and other unselfish breadwinners had to leave their family at home and take the Scottish Middle Class day trippers doon the watter to Rothesay, Dunoon and round the Kyles of Bute.

But to me, Drung was our nearest town, where I had been baptised - where the real shop was - Sean Di's - and a petrol station and the Church and Hugo's. Drung was where we walked to on a Sunday to go to Mass and meet up with relatives and friends on the bridge and down at the shore beneath the Royal Oak pub.

But Drung was nothing to Moville, Billy Doherty said. Moville was the place. That was where his dad and his uncles would take their punt and sail and win the cups – just as they did year after year with pride. Even my fiercely independent aunt Ellen over from America regaled me with her own stories of Sandy Doherty's exploits and successes every summer in his special Whitecastle punts. It was as if the Doherty's were winning for everyone up around Whitecastle and Ruskey and Crehenan.

So my curiosity was up and we sat around the lanes and fields at night, working out how we would take part in and win at the field races, the swimming in The Foyle and the five-a-side football. We even heard that Bobby Evans and Berti Peacock of Celtic and the magnificent Danny Blanchflower of Spurs would be playing in the Bay Field. The lure of it all was too great and our whole time was spent in planning our time, our route and our victories.

And everyone helped us in our dreams of glory. One of our neighbours, Willie Davenport, took us out in the evenings with his sons Martin, James and Eddie, with Paddie Joe Callaghan and a whole host of friendly faces I never even knew. And we raced and ran and tackled and scored goals and tried out tug – o - war until nightfall, with Rex the dog snapping playfully at our feet and our mother's voice calling us home.

On the great day of the regatta, we hitched a ride to Drung on my Uncle James's beautiful sky blue cart. Then my sister Bridget would go the rest of the journey with my Aunt Ellen in Sean Di's new van with Maureen, Stella and Carmel Doherty and their mum Peggy.

My own route was to be by sea - down the Foyle with my cousin Torrance who was proud at so young an age to be given the honour of taking the helm in the Smith's newly painted punt with his Uncle Jim. On a sunny but windy morning, Torrance steered the punt carefully down the coast past *The Black Point* at Redcastle, round the dangerous *Brown Shoulder*, skirted the dangerous hidden shallows along past *Claggan Shore* and majestically towards the pier at Moville.

As we skimmed along through the moored yachts and the rowing boats packed with day -trippers, we could hear the roars of the crowds and the shouts and the ever increasing sound of music. We had reached our goal and could barely wait to see what lay in store for us at the Moville Regatta that beautiful day which has embedded itself for ever in my memory.

The Bayfield was bursting at the seams as Torrance eagerly tied up the new punt to the edge of Moville pier and I scrambled up the iron ladder. I had known that although he had taken me with him in the punt, there was no room for me in any of the sailing events. He knew also that my mind was set on getting up onto the pier and into the crowds and noise and the roars of laughter and applause that echoed up Moville Main Street.

My first aim was to get up to the Bayfield where a torrid football match was in full swing. I raced up Quay Street and out onto the main road and across the bridge, weaving and dodging in among the crowds who were making their own way up the main street towards the Square. As I skirted the fields down on my left I got a clear view of the football and the surging, swaying crowd – going this way and that – just like a massive wave, keeping in time with the attacking team.

Further up the town, Moville Square was jam packed. Horses and carts and lorries and tractors all crossed and criss - crossed as they made their way up towards the fields at Lafferty's Lane for the horse racing or the ploughing. Hordes of youngsters, hair flying and eyes electric with excitement raced this way and that as their childish fancy drew them towards the stalls in the Church fields or across the Square. Others raced wildly down past Gerry Lynot's corner shop and down past the Prospect Hotel and out onto the Green.

Golden Days in Donegal

I had only seen the Moville Green from the distance of the Foyle as we had sailed majestically up towards Derry on the morning we arrived. Then, from the deck of The Lairds Loch that morning, the Green had looked so neat and measured and trim and empty. Now, as I came bursting out from around the Prospect Hotel, my eye caught sight of the Davenports and some of the other Ruskey boys racing along the edge of the cliff and down to the crowded pier. Their target was the starting point at the slipway - for the swimming race in the Foyle.

My heart raced as I realised I had a chance to shine in front of the very people I admired so much, but who knew nothing about me or my life. But I had one golden advantage from my Glasgow upbringing. I had one secret skill which I had never spoken about and had never had the opportunity to use as we passed our days high up in the hills up the Ruskey Road. Although it was normal to boast about friends and games and events back in Glasgow, we never really talked very much on holidays about life back in Scotland. We wanted it left behind.

The race which was marked out with rope on either side looked an easy one for me and I soon borrowed a pair of swimming shorts. About nine of us all around the same age were ushered into two large rowing boast and taken out as far as the bathing boxes. The day was glorious and the warm sun shimmered along the glistening Foyle.

As I stood on the edge of the boat waiting for the shout from one of the Committee to plunge into the water, a sudden hush came over the crowds sitting along the edge of the upper green and in the little bays along the shore. My mind raced back to an amazing film from back in Glasgow called ' Geordie ' where, after the hush, the athlete is roused to win the race by the sound of his girlfriend's voice – echoing from far, far away up the hills. As I waited and our heads dipped down to catch the very second that would start the race and get the slightest advantage, I heard her shouting loudly to me from the shore and just as her voice reached my ears, the shout went up. GO.

We were off the edge of the boat and into the cool water of The Foyle. As I swiftly eased myself into the crawl stroke I had practised so often back in The Public Baths in Maryhill, I knew I was going to be the winner of this Foyle race. As the others drifted behind my powerful stokes, I could see the slipway coming up closer and closer and the shouts of the crowds urged me on, faster and faster.

Before I realised it, I was out of the water, slithering up the slipway and rushing up the final slope into the arms of one of the race officials - my hands high up in the air in a victory salute. I turned and looked back and only them realised that I hadn't been as far in front of the rest of the swimmers as I had imagined. Fired up with the desire to win the race and get the applause from the crowds around the pier and the high rocks, I had exaggerated my lead to myself and had almost been caught by a boy from Culmore who was only two or three steps behind me.

But I had won - and all I could think of was racing through the crowds and over towards my friends who had cheered me on with undivided loyalty. I felt proud that she had seen me in my moment of glory. I was still too shy to rush over to her in such a crowd, and could only hope that she was proud of me and would be more attracted to me as we all gathered around the bridge at Drung later that evening.

My day in Moville that year at the Regatta, although I never took part in any of the big sailing events, was a day I would always remember. My pride was not only personal - to have won, but most of all to have pleased the crowd and won a race in front of the people I loved.And especially to have done so in the midst of the laughter and music on the shores of the glistening Foyle.

Golden Days in Donegal

I was delighted while writing my book to meet up with Patsy Cavanagh , one of Inishowen's best loved singers. His enchanting song about Moville helped me to realise that my own happy memories had been echoed in the beautiful words he wrote. To me, his song captures the joy and nostalgia we all feel as expatriates when we think back on those golden days of our Inishowen childhood. I am happy to share this with you as we go down memory lane together.

MY HOME TOWN OF MOVILLE

The evening sun is at my back , the city far behind me.
Each turn along that winding road brings memories to me still.
The summer's in her majesty , she's woke the yearning in me,
to spend a while with friends of old in my home town of Moville.

Out in the bay a tanker lay awaiting on directions.
The pilot left the Upper Pier to guide the stranger home.
And football teams in red and green were playing in The Bayfield.
I met a friend from yesteryear going down the River – Row.

Ah Moville, It's been a long time, it's good to be remembered.
I know that you can see my shadow standing in your square.
If the evening's fine , we'll take a walk and meet you at St Eugene 's.
We'll go down by Glenburnie and come up the shore from there.

Along the shore the fishing boats were making their way homeward.
Across the green the laughter of children at their games.
The spire of St Columba's split the sky up to the Northland –
an old man rested for a while at Ballynally Lane.

The evening sun is at my back , the city far behind me.
Each turn along that winding road brings memories to me still.
The summer's in her majesty , she's woke the yearning in me,
to spend a while with friends of old in my home town of Moville.

(c) Patsy   Cavanagh

Chapter 10

Bringing Home the Turf

My uncle Johnnie proudly displays the new turf which had been brought down from the hill that day. As precious as gold in the cold winter nights.

During our summer holidays, on bright summer afternoons, when we were taken high up through the twisting roads leading up to Glencaw hill, I experienced for the first time the magic of ' bringing home the turf'.

Looking along the banks of turf that dominated the edges of the rutted hill tracks created over the generations by our ancestors, I never failed to be humbled at how the people I loved and lived with had to dig and bring home their own fuel. It only dawned on me slowly in my idyllic summer Donegal holidays that, without the turf, they would have had nothing to heat the cottages and farms when the long and bitterly cold, winter winds blew down from the Inishowen hills.

To us back in Glasgow, coal, if you didn't have electric or gas fires, was delivered to your door in a large black sack by a soot covered delivery man. Regularly each week in sun or rain, Willie Anderson or Sandy McPherson would heave the coal -bag off the back of their lorry, onto their weary shoulders, hump it up the stairs and dump it in the kitchen bunker. If you were lucky and you lived up a tenement stair where the landings were wider, they would oblige and dump your parents' one or two bags in the bunker outside the door.

How different it was as the golden summer days passed in our Inishowen rural wonderland, where the dark tenement close, twisting staircases and rubble filled back gardens faded into the distance. Any thoughts of Glasgow disappeared as we raced joyously through our Ruskey fields and lanes and savoured the joys of playing endlessly with our Inishowen friends in a world of open sunlight and green grasses.

With the hypnotic, enchanting Foyle as a backdrop to our country landscape, any thoughts of Glasgow vanished - and as time passed, it was as if this was our only real world – a captivating, natural and safe world into which we were irresistibly drawn.

After our days playing and visiting and we sat round the table as night drew in, more and more talk was heard around the fire that the turf was ready to be brought in. I was always puzzled by the word 'turf' as I had never seen one or held it in my hand. The only time back in Glasgow I had heard the word was when our local church in Maryhill was having a new lawn laid using turf. But that was of course a totally different turf to what Uncle Johnnie and his neighbours had in mind – not smooth or green or for laying as an artificial garden or lawn.

To them 'turf' was one of the most precious things to come out of the ground. To them turf was as basic as clean water from a stream or spring well - or potatoes from a field or rushes from the moss to cover the cottage roof. The first time I ever handled a piece of turf I remember being amazed, despite my shock at its basic brown colouring and hardness, at the sudden feeling it gave me of something so basic and yet so fundamental to the everyday life of everybody in the area. It always gave my Uncle Johnnie a gentle but never ending sense of puzzlement and amusement that I should find any fascination with it at all!

Yet, it had always baffled me as to who had first decided what place our turf was to come from and had we paid for the area of mossy hill where the turf lay. Uncle Johnnie was never one for going into details about who got what first or who owned what. His simple life was too much dominated by the regular chores of his everyday struggle to make life tolerable and happy for himself and aunt Liza.

He only once in a casual conversation at night mentioned that his grandfather had told him that the McLaughlin piece of bog had been given to the family as a reward. However, although never one for dramatising anything or looking for praise, he revealed that it was given to one of his great uncles for saving the life of a one of the big landowner's son who had fallen into a deep trough one wet summer around the middle of the 19th century.

But to Uncle Johnnie and to his neighbouring small landholders and farmers, turf was like gold. As the summer days swayed from dry to wet to dry again, the only regular talk was about how and when to get the first turf down from the hill. Constant discussions and debates took place as to what was the right time to organise getting the turf down so that the fuel would be there to heat the home and cook the food through the long winter nights in the lonely Donegal hills.

My sister Bridget and my brothers never ever thought for a moment about there being no turf - or the weather being bad and ruining it as it lay by the bogside roads up on the hill. In our innocent and magically blinkered view, the turf was always there outside the cottage, day in - day out. We passed it every day, a re-assuring giant, half used up stack of dry turf positioned carefully at the top of the lane at the head of the cottage.

Uncle Johnnie in his usual simple, effective and practical way always constructed a clever shelter for his precious turf. He had, as my grandfather before him, carefully positioned it against the sheltered high west facing ditch at the top of the lane behind the cottage. The turf stack then lay snugly to the side of the slap into the field where the old people had built the original cottage over a century before. To cover the turf stack and protect it from rain and dampness, Uncle Johnnie had constructed a covering of old plastic, with rushes round the sides - and tied it strongly to the old wooden fence that ran along the top edge of the field.

We loved more than anything being sent out with the old battered bucket to bring in supplies of turf, especially in the morning when Aunt Liza would blow the cinders in the hearth and add a few sticks to get the fire burning and then add our turf into the range. We had never seen a range before and it had been the biggest thing bought by Uncle Johnnie and Aunt Liza after their marriage. Before that, as was still the case in the lower room, the turf had simply been put into the open hearth and arranged as a small stack with the kettle and the tea pot sitting on the small inshots, ready to be filled and poured a hundred times throughout the day.

We were fascinated that in other cottages nearby, along the rodden and up along the upper road, there was no range and the turf fire was right in the middle of the hearth. We marvelled at the way the turf was neatly stacked together with the flames leaping round them, the intoxicating waft of the smell of the turf in the air and the kettle on the crook hanging from the metal rod across the hearth.

So the actual bringing home of the turf was an event which to us was full of adventure, hard work and fascination. We had noticed that Uncle Johnnie had been making more regular short visits to the hill, leaving early in the morning and returning late at night. He was already up there in Glencaw, digging out the turf sods, laying them out along the edge of the road and then temporarily stacking them to catch the best of the sun and drying wind during the best of the weather. Uncle Johhnie, like so many of that wonderful generation of quiet, industrious folk, just got on with what had to be done, inviting no praise or publicity, but quietly getting the stack ready for the day when we would all pitch in together to make the first big haul.

I remember the preparations well – the quiet talk the evening before - and Aunt Liza preparing extra supplies of scones and tea and special cold meats she had bought on the Sunday after Mass from Sean Di's in Drung. My dad was still with us and he and uncle Johnnie had talked long into the night about getting the big haul of turf down the next day, and who would be helping and what would be the best way to organise it. My dad knew the importance of turf and of getting it home safely, often telling us how, as a boy in Connemara, he and his dad and brothers had to slog their way through the stony fields up into the hills with nothing but a donkey to bring in their turf. Uncle Johnnie was always fascinated to hear that in some other parts of Ireland, bringing home the turf was an even more difficult and demanding event than in his Inishowen hills.

As the sun blazed its way through the bedroom windows just after dawn, I remember hearing the familiar crunching of wagon wheels coming up the back lane. It was my godmother Bridget's brother, James, with his brand new, brightly coloured cart, with specially extended sides to make sure we got as much turf as possible for the long journey back.

No time was wasted as we devoured our bacon and eggs, packed our bags with Liza's special snacks and headed up to the crossroads to collect my mother's cousin, another Johnnie Mclaughlin, just known to us as Mannie's Johnnie.

It was a family affair and quietly and seriously James urged his beautifully decorated Clydesdale Nellie up the Crehenan Road and round the long right hand bend - and up towards the mosses and the harsh barren, rutted lane that straggled up to where the turf was stacked. The chat was quiet and jovial and I as I gazed regularly back down across the fields towards the ever widening Foyle, the two Johnnie's and James reminisced about days in their own youth when they, at my age had made the same essential journey.

Then, as uncle Johnnie later explained, there wasn't always a cart and the trip up for the turf was made on foot, guiding a horse with a donkey trailing on a lead behind. Once up on the hill, the task was to fill the bags for slinging over the side of the animals and heading back down to Ruskey. Then, after a short mid-day break they would head up again to complete another run and get back before the sun began to dim over Crehenan hill.

But now as we arrived at the ancient spot where the turf had been stacked for drying, we jumped down and began to fill the cart as speedily as we could. It would in Uncle Johnnie's view need another return visit the next day and the day after if we were to get in all he needed to keep the fires burning over the winter. While we threw the sods of turf up onto the cart, James, singing quietly under his breath, stacked and positioned them on the cart and made the slanted, supporting edges around the cart so that as much could be packed into the middle and up as high as possible. The decision as to when to stop packing was his and his alone - and he would judge where to position and place the last pieces of turf so that the balance was right and the load secure.

When James had decided that the load was just right, we all began to pack up our bags and jumpers and start to head back along the bog road and down towards Crehenan. With our backs and arms sore, but feeling a proud satisfaction that we had all worked as a team to get the first load onto the cart and on its way home, we filed in behind the cart and followed Nellie as she made her cautious strides along the rutted, dusty roads. To save his animal from strain, James had calculated the exact amount of turf and where it should be on the cart so that the journey down was easier for her - and she trotted obediently, head down, back along the road we had come up six hours earlier.

We all knew that it would be a long walk back down the hill, but were filled with an inner satisfaction that the first big turf haul of the summer had been cut, dried and now carted on its way down to the cottage. As they chatted quietly about their own younger days and we headed down behind Nellie, I couldn't help drifting behind a short distance and marvelling with pride and wonder at the simple, but determined ways in which they dealt with these everyday events of their lives in Donegal.

As we rounded the hill road that took us down towards the first houses at the top of Crehenan, I gazed at the broad sweep of fields and mosses that swept down towards the crossroads and Ruskey. As usual in my golden memories, the Foyle sparkled and glimmered in a hazy mid - day sun and my heart leapt with some inner, unfathomable feeling of being where I belonged - and with the people I loved most in the world.

Chapter 11

High Noon at Quigley's Point

My brother John rounds up Nellie for our Wild West Show at Quigley's Point Sports. He won't ride Nelly, but will sing out the words of the song 'High Noon'.

The day that Doctor McGurk asked me to organise a Wild West stall at the Quigley's Point Sports Day gave me a completely new insight into my summer holidays in Donegal.

Until that time, my days and weekends had been full of games in the fields with my friends, leaping over stacks of hay, vaulting hedges or racing from one cottage to the other to see who we could meet next. It was a time of unforgettable exuberance, fun and idyllic happiness.

We had been down at Drung that Saturday evening, as usual, meeting at Sean Di's and then cavorting about the petrol pumps and around the bridge. As the evening drew on we decided to play a game of hide and seek, using Hugo's Bar, the school, the bridge and the main door of the church as our bases.

We all had to come up with a game of our own, say what it was about, make the rules and get the game going. I remember the fun and amazement on my friends faces when I came up with a Scottish riddle to check out who would be 'het'. Whichever of us then was ' het' would decide where we could hide and how long we would have to find the others when they stole away into the evening glow to find a place to conceal themselves.

Anna, Torrance, Bridget, Maureen, Mickey Glackin, Carmel and Sean all stood back on the bridge as I shouted out the rules I had made up. I added a Scottish rhyme to the rules, and had had done so deliberately, so that I would impress them, especially Anna and look important and clever in front of my Irish friends.

In a broad Glasgow accent I shouted out:

> *Up the hill ' n*
> *doon the brae,*
> *that's the wey*
> *tae get away.*
>
> *Hide yirsel*
> *Behind a tree,*
> *But,*
> *If ah catch ye…*
> *Yi'll nivir get free.*

As usual, because I had made up this game, I wasn't ' het ' and when Anna turned her back on us to count up to 52 - and leaned against the side wall of Sean Di's shop, we were off like whippets – down towards the Master's house, round behind Hugo's and in my case up the steep, short hill that took you to the main front door of St Columba's Church.

As I raced up to the door and crouched down behind the pillar on the left, I could just barely see the frantic efforts of the others to get away into hiding before Anna had stopped counting to 52 –

one count for every week in the year. I pulled my body in close to the church door, my heart beating wildly and my whole attention in the world on keeping out of sight. My big hope was that Anna would take an easy route from the shop and head across the main road to Hugo's or down the lane that lead to Drung beach.

Long minutes past and nothing happened. I felt safe and calculated that Anna had gone for any easy 'kill ', one of the gang who had hidden nearby, in behind Hugo's wall or up the lane behind Sean Di's shop. As I rose slowly above the low wall to gaze down the church brae, a hand clasped me by the arm and I swung round in stunned amazement. My mind couldn't figure out how on earth Anna had sneaked up the brae and crept in to catch me from behind. As I turned to face her I thought that she must have pretended that she was heading for the shore and raced back along the Derry Road wall, skirted the graveyard and sneaked up on me. I threw up my arms in mock surrender and turned to face Anna whom I knew would be grinning with glory that she had tricked me at my own game.

When I turned round though, it wasn't Anna at all, but the smiling though astonished face of Dr McGurk. He had just closed the church up for the night after setting out the vestments and settings for Mass the next day and had come round from the side of the church to check that the front door was locked.

'And what's all this my young man ? '

He glanced down at me with a puzzled, but playful expression on his face.

'Ah, so you're the young man from Glasgow who keeps running around with your Hopalong Cassidy jersey, your imaginary rifle and pistol and - if I 've heard the tale right, sneaking rides on Charlie Grant's mare and the donkeys down on the shore field. '

I blushed, sputtered and stammered, embarrassed to the hilt that Dr McGurk of all people would find me crouching down behind the church wall in the evening haze outside the main church door. I wondered how this man could have any knowledge of so unimportant a person as myself who had only been in the area for a few weeks and only came to Drung for Mass on a Sunday or on sunny evenings to play. This was a person I was in total awe of and had only seen in his majestic church vestments saying Mass every Sunday. I stood back, just about to explain why I was there hiding and to apologise for giving him a fright. But he took the initiative and he spoke first, slowly, with his tongue in his cheek and a half smile on his chubby face.

' Right Stephen,' he said glancing down the brae as the others came racing up to find out what was happening.

' Since you're so fond of the church and you've so much energy at this time of night, I'd like you to help by running a Wild West stall at our Sports Day. You can help to bring in some funds for the church repairs and since you're so keen on being up near the church door at night, I'm sure you won't mind. They're not on for three weeks yet, so you'll have plenty of time to round up your posse, as I believe they say in all the best Wild West films.'

I had certainly shown more interest in horses and in riding then than either of my brothers Martin or John and took every opportunity to take James 's lovely black mare out and wash her down and groom her – if I got riding on her back up to the crossroads and back. I also remembered sneaking into the field as often as I could with a handful of carrots to where Charlie Grant's beautiful new foal was and petting her and feeding her.

The thought then suddenly flashed into my mind that Doctor McGurk must somehow have found out that it was me who had adopted the injured donkey up at my Davenport haven - and nick -named her ' Atomic Bomb' on account of the sudden, explosive kick she let out if anybody touched her sore side.

So now I had the honour or burden of responding to Dr McGurk's plea.

' We need some more of you young people helping us out,as well as our own parishioners, ' he said loudly as Anna and the others came racing up the brae, clearly wondering what the commotion was all about up at the church gate.

' Yes, Stephen, my boy. There's a fine posse of helpers and accomplices in front of you now. Tell them what my plan is and come back to me when you've all decided how you're going to make your Wild West Stall the biggest money spinner ever at the

Sports Day. The best in the West in fact ' he quipped as he turned down the brae, his long black robe swinging out behind in the evening breeze.

As Dr McGurk slowly made his way down the church brae, through the gates and into the shop, we stared at one another in a kind of amused disbelief and then in a kind of mocking roar, they all let rip, with Sean Doherty starting it off.

' Yup, sir. You're a gonna git a Wild West show on the road, cowboy.
An' you kin be the bossman - and we kin be yore deputeeeees.'

But it was no joking matter now and we abandoned our childish games at the thought of a request from the Priest and made our way in a serious stillness back down the church brae and into Sean Di's shop. The shop was a kind of magical world to us and a home from home. Sean Di knew that we hardly ever bought anything, other than the odd packet of sweets, but he and Peggy had a fantastic love of children and tolerated our constant, noisy meetings and games either outside the shop or inside if the weather was bad.

We huddled together beside the huge mirror that stood just to the right of the shop entrance. For some unknown reason, all of us had suddenly taken to the idea of organising and setting up a stall at the shows. As we discussed when the shows were and how we could get there and how we could set up a stall that would be the pride of the whole area, our minds became more and more active. It was as if the challenge from the priest had taken us out of the childish world of ' hide and seek' and ' tig' and made us realise for the first time that we could do something for the parish that would make us real heroes and not imaginary ones.

As the days passed leading up to the Sports day, we met and planned at every opportunity. I was to be the singing cowboy, with a wide - rimmed, white Stetson hat and red cowboy boots with noisy, jangling spurs. Anna was a fantastic source of outfits and props, secretly tracking down all kinds of costumes in the schoolhouse which her dad, the master, had used over the years in summer plays and winter pantomimes.

Charlie Grant up at Whitecastle would provide us with his

beautiful black mare as he was going up to Quigley's Point for the shows anyway. We now had a perfect horse on which I could make my dramatic, singing entry to the shows. Our biggest problem, however, was in getting a rifle for the shooting stall. Although we all lived or holidayed in cottages and farms across the Inishowen hills, nobody seemed to know of or at least admit that they actually knew anyone who had a gun. We all had heard rumours that there were guns hidden in farmhouses - up in the thatch or under old boxes in the out houses - but it always puzzled me that we still hadn't come up with a definite source for a gun as the days rapidly drew in towards the gala day.

But then it was all solved, and by a pure co-incidence. Bridget and I were down visiting old Jane when she told us that her son, Eddie – nicknamed Red Ned, had a real air rifle. Eddie used it to get rid of the rooks and crows that pestered his sheep and lambs in his own fields which were spread out down from Davenport's and almost the entire length of the whole lower Ruskey Road.

After our first meeting with Eddie, as he watched over his huge flock of sheep in the fields leading up to Mannie's on the upper road, *WE HAD REALLY STRUCK GOLD!* Eddie quickly agreed, not only to give us the loan of the brand new air-rifle, but said as a favour to us all that he would personally make up a special shooting gallery for the Sports Day.

He explained that he had seen one at a show in Belfast and that it had been a huge success as it gave everybody a chance to shoot through a small hole in the target board. If they were a reasonable shot – or even just lucky - and their shot cut the fine string that hung behind the hole, the string broke, a bell rang - and the biggest prize of the day was won.

Everything was now ready and the big day came when we got up early and the posse of our friends all met at the foot of the Ruskey Road. I was dressed up in my cowboy outfit and Charlie Grant had set off early with his lovely mare. Sean Di had agreed to bring his van and take us all up to the shows as he was going to be selling sweets and fancies there to the crowds who would come from all over the area.

When the big moment came, Sean Di let me off the van in the middle of the main street in Quigley's Point, just outside

Callaghan's Hotel and I met Charlie Grant at the petrol pumps where we had agreed he would have his mare all ready for my entry. As I leapt up onto the mare's bare back, and adjusted my holster and swung my legs over the back of the mare, I felt that I was the hero of the hour. The stall was all set up with a large carboard sign telling everyone what the prices were for shooting at the string and what the main prize was – a ten shilling note.

I nudged my knees into the mare's side and started singing out as loud as I could. I don't know where the words came from - or the courage – but my voice echoed down the street and I nudged the mare into a trot. As the crowds of people turned to gaze up the main street and see what the commotion was all about, I pulled out a pistol from my side holster and started firing the blanks into the air. At the sudden bangs, the mare got startled and flew into a gallop right along the street, into the field and in amongst the crowd who were just standing inside the main gate of the field where the shows were to take place.

Without realising what I was doing, or working out whether or not I could do it, I threw myself from the mare and rushed up to the top of the slope just inside the gate. As it suddenly dawned on me that I had made my dramatic entry and done my part – I gazed around to see who was at shooting stall. I had nothing to fear, for there they all were - my buddies from Ruskey and Drung, all bedecked in cowboy outfits, hands on their hips waiting for the word to start the show.

As the crowds started to move up towards the stall and get their chance to win the star prize, my brother John started to sing his favourite cowboy song at the top of this voice. And as the strains of ' Do Not forsake me, O my daaaaarlin' echoed down the hill, the crowd stopped and started to clap, and I rushed out to offer the air-rifle to the first person on the scene who wanted a shot.

And there he was, my own uncle Johnnie.

Never having said he would be there, he knew how important it was that our young group could make a success of the day - and had made sure he would be there to fire the first shot at the target. As uncle Johnnie leaned on the table we had set up and took aim, my brother John's voice got louder and louder and the strains of the words of the song from the film High Noon echoed down from the stall and right in amongst the crowds who were waiting to follow in Uncle Johnnie's footsteps.

Uncle Johnnie's three shots, much to my delight, didn't break any string and I knew he had just taken his bold step to get the thing started and hadn't really aimed for the kill. As the day went on and our singing and shouting drew in the crowds, the competition grew fiercer by the hour as nobody seemed able to snap the tantalising piece of string.

At last, however, as we were beginning to run out of pellets for the gun, a small, soft hatted, red haired man from Muff walked up - put down his money and took one long aim. The echoing piiiiing from behind the hole after his one and only shot let us know that the game was up and the string had been broken. He said nothing, put out his hand and I slipped the crisp note into it. He nodded his head and strolled off into the crowd, leaving us all gazing at one another in astonishment.

Our great consolation however, apart from the sheer fun we had at getting the stall up and playing our part in the church fund raising, was that we had taken in the most money ever for the parish on that day. Long after we packed up our stall and headed home down the Foyle, we talked and boasted about it proudly as the day we had our own high noon at Quigley's Point – without ever firing a single shot in anger.

Chapter 12

Neil Smith's Cadillac

In all our journeys from Derry to Ruskey and around the countryside during our holidays, nothing ever compared with the times we were met at the quayside by Neil Smith from Drung in his 1948 Chevrolet limousine. Neil was my mother's cousin and was one of the most placid, calm and laid back man we had ever met.

On those joyful days when we stood on the deck of the Laird's Loch as she swung round at Derry and edged into the quayside, we were never sure whether or not Neil would be there at that time in the morning or had been out salmon fishing all night or had booked first by someone else. If he knew in advance that my mother was coming over with her wee ' Scots tribe', as he called us, he would even give up another hire to be there to take his cousin and her family swiftly down the Derry to Moville Road and up the road to Ruskey and our holiday haven in the Hills of Inishowen.

But my heart leapt with joy the first time I ever saw him waving up to us as we clung to the railings of The Laird's Loch the year before. As the ship swung round in the Foyle that day and berthed at the quayside we couldn't wait to get down the gangplank, past the sheds and into the luxury of the leather seats in his Cadillac. As we sank into the soft leather after a night on the hard seats and decks of the Lairds Loch, we knew that we would have no trailing of cases along the quayside and up to the depot to wait for the first Derry to Moville bus.

We felt so proud and important as we watched hundreds of our fellow travellers who had shared the night with us, head up into Derry in the misty dawn to wait for buses to take them on the final part of their journey. But as Neil quietly slid our bags and cases into the giant trunk of the car, we cast sympathetic glances towards the droves of fellow travellers who were coming down the gangway and heading off in all directions to catch other public connections to take them to Carndonagh or Letterkenny or Buncrana or Falcarragh.

Everything inside the car was luxurious and soothing to us, from the leather of the seats to the window handles to the plush red carpet on the floor of the car. As Neil quietly tucked us in to the backs seats and then slid quietly into the driving seat, he gave a re-assuring nod of welcome to my mother and switched on the engine. We slumped back and the car purred its way up from the quayside, right along through the streets of Derry along past the Guildhall and and into Culmore Road. We knew it was now a straight road towards Muff and Ture and down into Quigley's Point and then on to Ruskey.

Derry was majestic that morning, with a golden sun breaking out early and clearing away the cold, early morning mist. We knew that our journey would be short now and once past the customs of Muff, we would soon be gliding along in our adopted Cadillac down past The Ture Inn, towards Greenbank Hall with the Foyle glistening on our right.

It seemed hours now since we had come up past the Ture Light on the Laird's Loch but we were now heading in the other direction – home- back down the Foyle – towards our cottage in the hills. The funny feelings we had experienced in our legs with having been at sea all night had left us and we gazed out at the Foyle, almost oblivious to the fact that we had been out there on the Scotch boat only a couple of hours earlier.

My sister Bridget very quickly fell asleep in the car that morning and I tried to take in every little piece of the Donegal names and place and landmarks as we glided along in Neil's car. Now awake after her night's fitful sleep on the journey over from Glasgow, my mother's joy at being back home was obvious as she chatted to Neil and caught up with all the latest family news.

As they reminisced about old times as they past the church at Iskaheen and the old schoolhouse at Quigley's Point, I tried again and again to get a word in as quietly as I could - and ask as much as I could about the origins of the words Ture and Iskaheen and Ruskey.

As Neil quietly and calmly leapt to my mother's defence he constantly diverted the childish questions away from her by pointing this way and that towards road signs and old cottages and some of the standing stones we past on the way down towards Quigley's Point. I was fascinated by all this and Neil regaled me with his explanations of the thousand and one question I was bombarding him with as he drove along

With the Foyle now closer and closer on our right and the first signs of activity in the roadside houses and down at the shore, I savoured all the sights we had longed to see all winter when the cold, winter days engulfed the streets and lanes and we longed for the first signs of Spring. Only then did we feel that the summer days in Glasgow would go in quicker and we would once again be closer to our journey back to Inishowen.

As we whizzed past the roadside cottages and gates and swung down from Quigley's Point towards the foot of the Crehenan Road, I caught sight of the big house standing proudly and defiantly on the shore at Whitecasle.   As we passed the famous old gates that had led down the now unused lane, my body quivered with excitement at all the things we would be doing again in our beloved fields and hills, houses and farms.

Suddenly, Neil was declutching and our magnificent Cadillac was slowing down and swinging hard left and up the bottom brae of the Ruskey Road. As the road narrowed and swung left and right, and his eager eyes made out the pot holes, Neil soon had us up past my uncle Dan's empty cottage and Willie Harrigan's brand new bungalow.

Passing the Barr's house on our right, he swung the car swiftly round past Maggie's shop and my godmother Bridget's cottage. Neil knew all the local roads like the back of his hand and he was soon leaning out his side window to negotiate slowly past the huge boulder that jutted out from the shugh at the opening to the rodden that ran along the field in front of our cottage in the hills.

Smoke billowed up from the newly painted chimney head and the barking of one of Aunt Liza's Collie's could be heard as it raced headlong down the field. I could see Aunt Liza now, her apron flapping in the gentle breeze, waving frantically at both her Collie and at the same time towards us, signalling that she was on her way to the foot of the lane to meet us and to get hold of the Collie before it raced out in front of Neil's car to attack the tyres on his car.

Although delirious to be at the cottage and seeing the smoke billowing up from the chimney and the familiar shouts of Aunt Liza as she came racing down the lane, we were almost reluctant to get up and ease ourselves out of our luxurious, leather seats. But Neil slipped the back doors open, gave a gentle signal to us to help him and we swung ourselves out to take the bags and cases out of the boot so that my mother could go straight to meet Aunt Liza.

There were too few occasions unfortunately when we had the luxury of being driven in style on our summer holidays, but despite that I can remember the joy of them all as if it were only yesterday. I think much of the magic of these memories was not only that we revelled in the sheer comfort of Neil's car, but he was such a calm, knowledgeable person that the very thought of being driven about by him was as pleasure. Neil made you feel that you were the most important person in the world as you glided through the roads and lanes of the Inishowen hills.

One journey in particular I remember was when my aunt Ellen – on one of her unheralded visits back from America, decided to take us all to her cousin Peggy's café in Derry. Peggy was related to us through my mother's mother whose maiden name was Smith. My uncle Johnnie explained to us that when my grandmother and grandfather got married - a Smith to a McLaughlin - all of the folk in the two families came together to help the young couple set up their own new cottage in Ruskey.

It was no short journey then, as my grandmother's Iskaheen home was on the other side of Scalp mountain, through the Grainne Gap, on the road to Buncrana. In those days at the start of the 20th century, there were no cars or lorries and our ancestors had to bring everything by horse and cart to help the young couple start their new life.

Uncle Johnnie told us that not only did the two families help with the moving of basic furniture and clothes to the new home – but they helped to actually build the cottage from the stones of the derelict, half - collapsed cottage in the field at the top of the lane.

This old cottage had been ravished during the evictions in the 1880's and once the roof supports had been taken away, and the old people moved into other family cottages and barns, ill health, deaths and the ravages of the Inishowen winters had reduced the old cottage to a pile of rubble.

But it was with pride and determination that my grandfather as a young man -and my grandmother as a new bride - saw the two families salvage the best of the stones and beams and build a brand new cottage during the early summer of the year they were married. It was as if the families were making a statement that, out of the rubble of the old sad days of evictions and strife, new life and new generations would come to live again with dignity and purpose in the shadow of the old, devastated home.

Neil Smith and Uncle Johnnie had a great affinity for each other and Neil was delighted the day he was taking us to Derry for a trip because Johnnie and Liza would come along. This was a big day out for Johnnie and Liza and they had to make sure that all the essential tasks around the house could be left for a whole afternoon. So, Neil came early and took my sister, my mother, brother and I on our own, giving Johnnie and Liza another hour or so to get themselves ready.

To both of them, the ride in Neil's Cadillac to Derry called for the greatest preparation and the ironing of the best clothes they could find. I remember Uncle Johnnie proudly showing off the one and only new suit he had at that time, the one he had bought in Carndonagh for his wedding to Liza ten years or so before. To Liza, the trip to Derry was also a great opportunity to discard the everyday working clothes and painstakingly and lovingly search through her wardrobe for what she considered to be her best dress, coat, handbag and shoes.

As we glided along towards Derry, our minds were on the day ahead and although we always wanted to be heading away from Derry down the road towards Ruskey and our cottage, we had no worries that day that we would be heading for the quay, the gangway and the long journey back to Glasgow.

Neil was an encyclopedia of information about the whole area and clearly enjoyed answering the barrage of questions we could fire at him about the places we passed through. On this particular journey, Neil swung the Cadillac hard right at Quigley's Point, at a place called 'the Carn Brae' just at McKeever's shop. As he drove along up the hill towards Carndonagh, he told my mum that he would   take a longer, slightly different route out towards a place called Glentogher - towards where some of my grandmother's people had come from.

As he drove past a range of hills on our left, he slowly gave us their names and we sat back taking the names in   : *Crockglass, Leamacrossan, Glackmore* and *Crocknacraddy* – all magical names to us, more mystical when pronounced by Neil in his quiet inishowen tongue as he eased round every twist and turn in the road with ease. Further up the road, Neil swung off to the left this time, at a place called Glentogher and immediately pointed out the magnificent sight of Inishowen's highest peak, Slieve Sneacht. As we asked him to say it out to us again and again, the words sounded more and more mysterious and we repeated it in our own way as Sleeve Snacht in unison, Neil nodding his head in sympathetic praise.

As we headed quickly down the road towards Buncrana, we just sat back in awe at the hills and   fields and sparkling streams around us and   listened in silence to the fascinating pieces of folklore and stories which Neil had for almost every mile along the road. Our journey through Buncrana and in towards Derry that day will always stick in my mind. It was the first time I had ever been through the hills from Ruskey going to Derry. Our normal Derry journeys were always short affairs, straight up the main Moville – Derry Road, whether in delight at having arrived for our idyllic holidays, or in dejection as we headed back up the road to the quayside, The Lairds Loch and our journey home,

I was always fascinated by my cottage views of Lough Foyle and the County Derry coastline, with the city of Derry at the top of the Lough, especially with her lights shimmering in the dark evening skies. But my memory of that journey through Buncrana and Fahan, skirting Lough Swilly to Burnfoot and then onto Derry, gave me a new and exciting panorama of a part of Inishowen which I would only discover in detail in later years.

And of course as we approached Derry our whole attention was on who would be there at Peggy's café - and what it would be like and which of our cousins would be there to share our delight at the journey we had just experienced in the luxury of Neil Smith's Cadillac.

Chapter 13

Bayfield Bedlam

Stephen waits for Willie Davenport's secret football practice. The bayfield is empty now, but will be packed for the matches on Sunday.

Although most of my Donegal friends all lived high up in the Inishowen hills and had to constantly work at the hay and turf and herding cattle - we found a hundred games and activities to play at during the long summer evenings. One of the most enjoyable times I had was when we all gathered about eight O'Clock in the evening in the field behind Willie Davenport's house and ran about in a wild, joyous pack playing at football on the sloping field that ran down towards upper Drung. There, on warm sunny, seemingly endless summer days, my brother John and I would race to the Davenports to see who would be coming along each evening to play.

We knew well that most of our pals had been out in the fields or up the hill from the early dawn, bringing in the hay or the turf for their own family. Some of them were even out ' on hire ' to the bigger, local landowners and farmers – like the Quigleys, Hancocks and Gourlays.

It took us some time to realise that, even in our seemingly idyllic world, our friends, although out of school for the summer, were not on holiday as we were. We didn't realise for some time that to their parents, the hard and relentless slog of tending the cattle and sheep and weeding the rows of cabbage and lettuce had to be done – and all the family were involved. In most families the work had to be done by everybody - no exceptions unless through illness - with each member of the family giving their best effort, especially when the weather was good and the sun blazed down on the fields and meadows.

It was easy for us to forget that the struggle to make ends meet for most of our friend's families was a constant reality – a perpetual battle to bring in enough food to eat, water to drink and turf to heat the home. To us it was pure fun and delight to be sent to the well for a bucket of water, or to take bottles of tea and newly baked scones up to the fields to Uncle Johnnie. All these tasks to us were so different from everyday life back in Glasgow. So we relished the chances we had at different times in the day to be sent to the upper or lower fields as Uncle Johnnie worked away tirelessly to cut, gather and stack the hay.

I can still see a vivid picture of him in the upper field, with his left hand firmly grasping the small handle of the scythe and his right arm swinging the long, curved, sharp blade through the blossoming hay, from left to right and back again - in a thousand careful sweeps. There was a lovely smooth action about his movement, his feet firmly splayed out to keep his balance and his hands lightly, but decisively clasping the long, twisted stem of the scythe.

Often, as he moved relentlessly along the part of the field he was cutting, he would hum out his favourite song, quietly recalling it to his mind and renewing the memory of one of the old songs of the hills which he had heard his own father sing when he was a boy.

The singing was more to help him keep in time with the swinging action and his constant, but deadly accurate action, saw him cut through swathes of hay in one area of the field. He would then move swiftly further down or across the field – depending on how he had decided to get the job done and to allow aunt Liza and ourselves to pick up the sheaves and stack them well away from the dangerous thrust of the scythe.

But our Inishowen friends didn't see the same magic or enchantment in the work in the fields - whether it was for their own family or out to earn a meagre wage to bring home on a Friday evening. To our friends these were only a few of the strength - sapping, monotonous, but essential daily chores they had to perform day in day out – whatever the weather.

I suppose this was why our pals came from all over the Ruskey, Crehenan and Drung homes to join in the evening football matches. We were amazed at the numbers who came on horseback and tractor and bicycle – all heading towards the same rough, slanting field where our football practices took place.

It was only when Willie Davenport brought us all together one evening and told us about a football tournament in Moville that we realised that we were training and playing for something big. Willie was a thoughtful, enthusiastic trainer and organiser - and made sure that the practices never got out of hand and that rules were obeyed. Willie was always there, having just come back from his own farming jobs, getting his dinner and organising the family chores for the next day.

It was always a delight to us that, although the games were not for shrinking violets and that you had to be ready to swerve and jump to avoid a sliding tackle or thudding shoulder, the wild enthusiasm seldom deteriorated into anger or fights. As the action swung back and forth across the field and the goals thundered in and the shouting increased in ferocity, Mrs Davenport would always seem to appear at the right moment with welcome drinks and thick pieces of buttered or jammed scones. We hardly took time however to stop and eat in any normal way, but chewed and drank as we raced and tackled and sent the ball roaring into the evening sky.

Most of our Donegal friends knew little about the street game of football that we played back home in Scotland. To them Gaelic football was the norm in their school, in their family and throughout the County. It seemed to us that, once they agreed that you couldn't handle the ball or scoop it up into your hands or punch it with your fist, they were every bit as good as we were.

Willie, wise coach that he was, would often stop the games at their height and get my brother and I to explain the intricacies of offside or throw - ins and convince our friends that we would gain nothing in Moville if our shots were blasted high over the crossbar to score a point as in Irish football.

Of course to us, Moville was far beyond our daily journeying. With no car and often no money to pay the fare to board a bus down the road to Moville, it was somewhere down the Foyle that we now might be visiting for the first time on our summer holidays. We knew from our parents that Moville was the big town in the area, apart from the big city of Derry up in the North. But their stories of Moville always seemed to be tinged with a kind of sadness, as they always told about the brothers and sisters and family and friends of their own age who had gone to Moville on a one way journey to America. In those days in the mid fifties, the memories and experiences of our Irish families were filled with stories of Foncie and Hugh and Mary Anne who had all gone on the long, lonely journey to Moville pier to take them to a new life and some money and a purpose in life across the Atlantic.

Moville to them was always to do with a sad crowd on the pier as the tenders carrying the passengers made their way out and back to the ships lying anchored at Moville Light. Moville was all about the Anchor Line ships and the packed tenders snaking their way out past the Lighthouse to the channel where job - hungry relatives, neighbours and friends would board the waiting ships.

But to our younger minds, the thought of going to this place called Moville was exciting and was not tinged with any sadness or depressing history. This was a first for our soccer team from Ruskey. Willie had arranged that we would all be taken by lorry to the town the following Sunday after Mass and that we would be collected on the bridge at Drung just after one O'Clock.

You can imagine the excitement we all felt that morning as we poured out of Mass and roared down the brae from the church and out onto the bridge outside Hugo's. Then, racing down the lane to the shore, we scrambled in behind hedges and haystacks and boulders to quickly change into the football shorts and tops Willie had borrowed from someone in Culdaff for the game. Calmly making our way up the shore lane again and passing a ball between us, we felt in some way like heroes, as we thought everyone passing from Mass was looking over at us and giving us a feeling of great importance.

As the lorry drew up and we scrambled into the back of it for the journey down to Moville, I caught the sight of Anna and her father, the Master at Drung school. I felt a hundred feet tall in my green and white football gear as I waved back wildly and the lorry edged in and out of the massgoers making their way out of Drung and along towards the Red brae or further down the road to Clar and Redcastle.

We, of course, had no time to stop for casual passangers and were too important to stop and give anyone a lift, for our minds were on the game down at the Bayfield in Moville. We had heard so much from Willie now about it and that it had real goal posts and nets and that there would be a large Sunday crowd gathered to watch the games in the various Cups.

Willie was immersed in football and could tell us all about a whole number of teams from magically sounding places like *Carrowmenagh* and *Clonmany* and from as far away as *Derry* and *Buncrana*. I was delighted at how often he repeated the name of so many McLaughlins who played for different teams, giving me at least one affinity with this new competitive world I was entering. As the lorry moved rapidly down past Redcastle Post Office and round the twisting bends that took us nearer and nearer to Moville, a nervous silence surrounded us and we talked in small groups in whispers, working out moves and tactics.

For once, I can remember not even being aware of the journey or the sun glimmering along the banks of the Foyle as we passed Clar and down the long, steep hill towards Carrickarory Pier. As the lorry swung round past the pier, we were shocked out of our quiet reflections on the game by a roar from the Bayfield just ahead of us.

What a sight met us as the lorry swung in the top gate and down to behind the goal at the town end of the Bayfield. There seemed to be hundreds of footballers, maybe eight or ten different teams in an array of colours : reds and purples and greens and blues. There were different minor football competitions too – all leading up to a cup final later in the afternoon.

Willie eased us through the crowds of people lining the field and told us to wait at the shoreside of the field until he came back with the arrangements for our own games. He had entered us in a number of five - a – side games and we would be representing Drung and Ruskey. He impressed on us that this was the first time an organised team had come down from Whitecastle and that much more successful and experienced teams had been coming for years and had done their own townlands proud.

What Willie had never been able to prepare us for was the bedlam of noise that would erupt as each new team took their places in the five a side games.

We had been so used to the regular cluster of players up on the fields up above Drung and the same faces and voices. We had become so used to the one rough, sloping uncrowded field, that the mass of people on every side of the Bayfield hindered, rather than helped our efforts to get into our planned game.

We had not realised either, despite all Willie's coaching and advice, that the games would be short ones, I think ten or fifteen minutes each half. As we tried to take our time and play the slower, more careful football we had practised, we were caught out quickly by faster, stronger, more attack minded teams.

We did manage in our second and third games to score some goals as we became more accustomed to the speedier play and the roaring of the Moville crowds, but we never got through to the final stages of the tournament and didn't get the chance to show how we could really play in a longer match.

It was an amazing feeling though to be applauded by such a huge crowd for the first time in our lives - and then to get the chance to relax on the edges of the Bayfield and watch the other senior games taking place amidst the roar and sway of the crowds.

I would never forget that chaotic but unforgettable experience and to have enjoyed the company of so many unknown McLaughlins, Dohertys, O' Kanes and others from all over Inishowen and beyond. Willie consoled us on our dignified, but ultimately unsuccessful efforts in the maelstrom that was the Bayfield on that glorious summer afternoon - and assured us we had done great credit to him and to our own townlands.

As we drove slowly back up past Carickarory Pier and round the bend out of the town, we all vowed as friends to get back as soon as we could to the bedlam and magic of football in Moville's Bayfield.

We didn't go many long journeys during our school holidays and our world mainly revolved around Ruskey, Drung and Quigley's Point. As we looked out of our cottage door in the morning we surveyed the new world we were part of and tried to put some kind of natural boundaries to it. It was so new and exciting to us, never before having been part of what to us was a vast landscape of hill, field and sea.

At times we found the change in environment overpowering. To have come from the cramped, hard streets of Glasgow to the soft, comforting fields of Inishowen was a complete, but deliriously happy culture shock. We often tried to compare our two worlds, but not for long, as our whole aim in life was to savour every moment of each day in our Donegal paradise.

Most of the time we were involved with close friends and neighbours in that neat and cosy little triangle of land – with Ruskey at the centre of our world and Drung down on our left and Quigley's Point up the Foyle on our right. Nor did we seem to have any great ambitions to go outwith our world.

We felt exhilarated with simple activities and tasks, like going to the well for drinking water or down the road into the mossy field and across to the river to haul up an endless supply of washing up water for Aunt Liza. Back home in Glasgow, we simply turned on a tap in the sink and that was it. The idea of having to carry buckets of water up the lane to the cottage, often spilling half of it in our excitement, was a magical, new feeling. Somehow, we never really considered what the water was needed for, but simply wanted to get on with some other task that would hopefully take us down to the Barrs or Bridgets or across the rodden to our friends.

It was a huge surprise to us when one misty summer morning, Neil Smith came out of the blue and asked us if we wanted a run that day to a far off town called Carndonagh – away at the other side of Inishowen. I don't remember much about Carndonagh that day, but I do remember the Diamond and the market stalls and going up into the Cathedral with Neil and my mother.

Carndonagh seemed an isolated, protective little town, nestling among hills with no loch beside it like Moville or boats nestling in a harbour. The people were just as friendly as back home in Ruskey or Moville or Quigley's Point, but there was something different about them – something mysterious to me which I tried to put down in this short poem – to show how I felt that day
My Poem : Carndonagh August 1955

Carndonagh!

Is that your name ?
Doesn't matter –
It's all the same !

Carn for short,
Carndonagh for long.
Tell me a story,
Give me a song.

Church on the height, at the head of the town
Standing for ages - Your glorious crown.
Where masses and prayers pour up to the sky:
At weddings and funerals, when the dear, old folk die.

From Carrick and Milltown and out to Drumaville.
We've heard of your fame from Derry to Moville.
Someday I will visit your old market square
And join in the fun at your proud summer fair.
Then onwards I'll travel, on a bright sunny day,
Out through Carndonagh to Trawbrega Bay.

Chapter 14

Thatching Days

My aunt Liza admires her beloved Johnnie's thatching and the new, neatly stacked winter supply of turf.

The very idea that anyone would put straw or reeds or any kind of thatch on a roof was a complete mystery to us, coming as we did from the high, slate – roofed, gray tenements of Glasgow. These were solid rock buildings, row after row, street after street – some old and crumbling like at the foot of the old Kelvindale Road or like our own tenement - only up fifteen or so years and sparkling new with golden roughcast finish and newly painted staircases.

The only time we ever had any occasion to look up and see what was on the roof was when we played 'ba 'ower the roof' from our narrow, railing enclosed backcourt. The aim of this 'roofy game' was to either throw or kick the ball as hard and as high as you could, up past the neighbours windows and over the roof. The whole purpose of this was that whoever was your partner would stand eagerly on the other side of the tenement, out on Kelvindale Road and across at the barracks wall for a good view, waiting for your shout to rush and catch the ball. The great challenge of course was to get the ball clearly up and over the roof with one kick or throw. But even if you just managed to reach the top and bump the ball over the other side, then your partner had to rush and catch the ball before it hit the pavement. If they did, you got the points and they had the pleasure of doing the same - only in reverse - so that you could catch it before it hit the backcourt. Then it all started over again. And that was our total and limited interest and knowledge of roofs in our Glasgow tenements.

You can imagine our surprise and puzzlement when we first saw uncle Johnnie and aunt Liza looking up uneasily at the inside of the cottage roof and talking seriously about the roof needing new thatch. We knew that this was no roof game they were talking about and we didn't need a second invitation to see what was involved. We were desperate to find out if there was any way we could help. It wouldn't have mattered to us if it was simply going up to the moss to gather reeds and long grass, or getting the chance to hold a ladder or take away the old thatch to burn it down at the river. We would gladly do anything to be part of the ritual that they both were going through and which we knew was as important to them as saving the hay or bringing home the turf from the Crehenan hill.

In fact, the decision to thatch the roof had been an easy one to take that year. Although Uncle Johnnie told us that he wouldn't normally be doing the thatching for another winter or so, he had been forced to change his mind and fit another time - consuming task into his busy summer days. He explained to us that the weather had been very bad in Inishowen during the previous winter, with un - naturally strong and persistant gales howling up from the Foyle or down from the snow covered, wintry wastes of Glencaw and Crehenan hills.

Of course we found it all hard to imagine in our minds that the soft, gentle hills we gazed out at each morning in our summer cottage could be stark, barren and un-inviting places. Also, when we thought about, or looked down at the Foyle, it always seemed to be shimmering in the sunlight and adding a picturesque tranquil, sea - backdrop to our idyllic landscape haven in the hills.

Uncle Johnnie, Aunt Liza and their neighbours, relatives and friends knew better. They were there all the year round in bitter, icy blasts and in dark November gales. Unlike us in our magical summer world, they lived in a real, relentless rural world – not just in the hypnotic, idealistic golden days of our summer, when the corncrakes always sang and the sun glimmered benevolently along the shores of the Foyle.

That was our world – a world that shut out all but the very slightest of awareness of the harsh realities of the world they lived in. In a way, perhaps because of how enchanting we wanted our world to be, we shut out any of these harsh realities. We preferred to glide innocently through a magical mist of sun and laughter and stories and journeys – happiness always enveloping our long days and carefree hours.

Uncle Johnnie, in his usual, thoughtful way, would only allow us a limited involvement in anything so important and demanding as thatching the roof. We were delighted of course and committed as we were, gladly volunteered to go with them up to the moss and gather in newly cut reeds and hay. As uncle Johnnie calculated the number of new bundles that were needed and we filled barrows and wheeled them excitedly down the road and up the lane to the cottage, we felt in some unknown way that we were part of an important event in preserving the very fabric of the cottage we loved so much.

On the day of the thatching, aunt Liza, probably wanting to encourage us to be away from the cottage while uncle Johnnie got out his tools and got organised for the actual work, sent us on an errand down to uncle Dan's house at the foot of the Ruskey Road. It was an unimportant, uncomplicated errand to collect a paintbrush which aunt Francie had borrowed now that they were back from Glasgow and starting to do up their cottage for their summer stay.

We raced away as usual, anxious to meet two more of the relatives we rarely saw, delighted that they were now over from Glasgow and offering another home to visit on the long summer nights. As we turned down the road away from our own cottage, we could see uncle Johnnie standing out on the cobbled, cottage yard, staring thoughtfully up at the thatch roof.

An hour later, as we came roaring back up past Barr's house, a paintbrush in each of our hands, we swung round into the rodden at the foot of the field in front of the cottage. And as we clambered excitedly over the ditch at the foot of the field, we could see Uncle Johnnie in all his glory up on the thatch roof. We raced as fast as we could, wondering how he had got up on his own and fascinated that we would see once and for all what all the planning had been about.

We scampered across the front field, and round into the front street of the cottage, shooing away the hens and geese who were cluttering and clustering around the half door, hoping that aunt Liza would appear with a bucket to throw them some scraps to eat. We stopped abruptly in our tracks just outside the cottage, and gazed up at the roof and were amazed at the sight we saw. Uncle Johnnie smiled down at us and we caught a glimpse of all the technology and scientific thinking that had gone into his scheme to thatch the cottage.

The first thing we noticed was that he had positioned a whole array of tools in a line along the top of the thatch, each strategically placed by him for the task he would do as he moved along the thatch. There was a claw hammer and a bucket of old nails and a small hand scythe, all placed within his reach so that he could move along and make use of each of them as they were needed.

Along the whole length of the roof, he had carefully positioned small bunches of the newly cut moss and hay which we had helped him fetch and carry from the fields down along the river. What amazed us most though, as well as all the tools, was the thick rope which he had slung firmly around his waist and which stretched high up over the thatched roof down towards the lane behind the cottage.

Much to uncle Johnnie's amusement, although at no time did he stop edging along the thatch, carefully pulling out old, sodden clumps of thatch and quickly replacing them with newly cut ones, we raced headlong round the head of the cottage and halfway down the lane - so that we were parallel to where uncle Johnnie was up on the roof.

And there it was, swinging gently to and fro, as he moved with experienced ease along the thatched roof, a huge boulder at the end of the rope which he had tied tightly and securely round his waist. He had not learned this scientific balancing act, however, as we might have done at school, in any scientific book or educational manual. For, as my mother had often reminded us, uncle Johnnie had not had the luxury of staying at school after his twelve birthday. From some deep instinct within him he had watched and learned how it was to be done from his own father and uncles over the early years of the century. This natural, unsophisticated education had taught him that the trick wasn't just to get up on the roof, but to use primitive but highly effective scientific principles to ensure that his balance was always kept right - and he was totally safe from falling to the ground and causing himself some critical injury.

As he moved slowly along the thatch roof, repairing and renewing as he went , any jerky or unsteady movements of his body posed no danger to him. If his feet slipped on the strap of wood that ran along the bottom edge of the thatch, the boulder on the other end of his rope would react and support his weight and sudden movements. No mind bogling mathematical equation had been calculated for this by him and aunt Liza the previous nights under the light of the Tillie Lamp. No book had been studied by them to solve an equation for it - as we did at school. Their knowledge, which had been handed down from generation to generation, made sure that he didn't fall from the thatch onto the cobbled stones in the 'street' in front of the cottage.

We watched in amazement and awe as this quiet, uneducated man humbly put all his ancestral experiences and tradition into play and removed, renewed and trimmed the thatch. With no fuss, he moved effortlessly from one edge of the roof to the other, repairing the damage done by the ferocity of the winter gales that had driven down from the hills onto the old thatch.

Not content with repairing and renewing the old thatch, our uncle Johnnie pulled off his piece de resistance. He edged further along to the gable end of the roof, where the chimney was, and whipping out an old family painting brush, he stabbed it into a huge pail of whitewash and stroked the paint round all the corners of the chimney. With quick and accurate strokes, never once getting the slightest whitewash on his uncovered hands, he had the chimney head gleaming white in the afternoon sun.

As the flickers of straw drifted down from the roof onto our heads, he hummed gently and untroubled at his thatching tasks. Amazed, we moved back into the field in front of the house and marvelled at him as the sun edged round over his busy shoulders until aunt Liza came up the lane from the shop with the special meats she had ordered for his tea that night. Then, as the evening sun began to dip down over the hills, we went inside to help make up the special meal he was to have that night and sit out the two bottles of Guiness which my mother had bought him as a treat on the day he thatched the roof.

Chapter 15

Songs in the Hills

*The half - door is open and somewhere in the hills around our Inishowen cottage,
other friends and relatives welcome the Scotchies with songs, news and story.*

One of the most magical memories from my Inishowen holidays – and memories that come back again and again - was going out visiting round the cottages and farms of our relatives, neighbours and friends. This was something new and wonderful to us and brought a rich enjoyment to our lives and introduced us to the songs and stories of our Inishowen hills and shores.

As the long summer days drew in and we came back from playing on the shore at Drung or from special shopping at McKeeever's store in Quigley's Point, we couldn't wait to get back up the Ruskey Road and get out again – into the evening shadows and into another magical Donegal world.

We didn't really understand or really think too much about the deep meanings behind the words of most of the songs or the echoes of sad times they brought to the hillside cottage. We just enjoyed these moments in time as neighbours came in to gossip and sing - and the turf fire burned brightly against the hearth as the night stars faded slowly into the first, soft glow of the dawn.

We were happy to sit back in this magical, warm and comforting world where stories and songs and accordion music mingled magically under the ancient rafters. The songs and stories recalled the struggles and events which had dominated the lives of our ancestors in the long years since they had set up home in the hills of Inishowen. The songs always recalled memories of these amazing folk - the very people who had carried, shaped and nailed the rafters and beams together into roofs for the thatched cottages dotted all over the slopes of the hills.

Snippets of the songs – words, phrases and melodies - drifted into our young minds and remained as comforting refrains back in Scotland on cold, bitter city winters when the tenement streets were iced up - and nothing moved - and the hills and songs of Donegal were far, far away.

My uncle Johnnie relaxes with his American relative John McLaughlin. The melodian is at hand and the clock is at five past three. It could have been in the afternoon - or as the dawn was breaking !

Glasgow had then - and still does have - the friendliest and caring people in the world, but it was a world then so far apart from and alien to our country cottage. Nothing back home in Glasgow could compare to be sitting in front of the turf fire, the kettle dangling on the hook and the happy, chattering voices and singing echoing around the rafters.

Golden Days in Donegal

We went visiting of course when we were back in Scotland, but only on one or two occasions to our relations in the different parts of Glasgow in Ruchill and Townhead in the centre of the city. But I never recall the magic of going out regularly at night to anybody's house just to sit and talk and listen and be enchanted.

Even today, I can still recall bits and pieces in my mind and still hum them to bring back some of those distant, but never to be forgotten golden memories. Words that constantly comes into my mind at any time are those from my father's favourite song *My Lovely Irish Rose* and the echoes of the emotions and the sadness of that song have stayed with me all my life. If I shut my eyes I can still see so clearly the scene around the turf fire and my father reluctantly being coaxed to sing his favourite verses in his soft Connemara accent. His main motivation was to sing a tribute to his own Irish Rose, our mother and his own Mary, to whom he was devoted until the day he died.

My Lovely Irish Rose

A winding river winds its way close to an Irish home
To mingle with Trawbeaga Bay where flows the Atlantic foam..
T'was on a spot close to the spot where the river gently flows,
That I said farewell to my own dear girl, My lovely Irish rose.

Oh Carn fair beyond Compare I never will forget
Oh Carn fair beyond compare I think I see it yet.
From Moville Bay we sailed away just at the evening close
And I waved my hand to my dear old land
and my lovely Irish rose.
Oh Mary dear, I'm lonely here, without you all the while.
I miss your loving words of cheer and I miss your Irish smile.
Before I go to sleep at night, before my eyes I close.
I pray that God may guide you right – my lovely Irish Rose.

One of my mother's favourites and a song she never tired of hearing being sung by neighbours like Johnnie or James when they dropped in to visit us all was *The Homes of Donegal*. I suppose it has stayed in my mind because it was my mother's favourite and also because it summed up part of the magical appeal we all felt during those summer days that the doors were always open to us and we were always welcome, no matter what, to enjoy the warmth, affection and support from those wonderful people.

In many ways, the words of my mother's favourite song summed up everything that we felt about the small, rural world we had entered from the harsh concrete urban world of Glasgow. As Johnnie or James would slide back on the chair and stare at the glowing fire, we would all join in as they put on their best voice to sing their version of the words and make us feel that the song was being sung specially for us and us alone on that particular night!

My mother's favourite song -

THE HOMES OF DONEGAL

Oh I've just called in to see you all, I'll only stay a while.
I want to see how you're getting on, I want to see you smile.
I'm happy to be back again and I greet you big and small.
For there's no place else on earth just like -
the homes of Donegal.

I love to see your happy faces, smiling at the door.
The kettle boiling on the crook as I step up the floor.
and then to see prepared for me,
a shake-down by the wall.
For there's repose for weary wanderers
in the homes of Donegal.

These songs and other much sadder ones about emigration and loneliness and darker days were all mingled together in our young minds and transported us into another world. We were fired with joy and eagerness to go to other houses and feel the warm welcome as we came round to the back door or chapped on the dimly lit windows. As dusk was falling and the fields slowly grew silent, except for the distant lowing of a cow or the bleating of a sheep high up on the hill, we eagerly helped to tidy the house up after supper - and then rushed down to the lower room to attend to our appearance.

It was fascinating to us that there were no sinks in our cottage to wash up in. So we took our turn to use the large washing up bowl to smarten ourselves up and put on some of the new clothes our parents had saved up for to take us back to Ireland to meet their brothers, sisters, cousins and neighbours.

It didn't occur much to us that to my mother, our evening visits were opportunities for her to be proud of her children: their manners, behaviour and appearance. We never really thought that, as we excitedly went into other houses and farms that we were mixing with the very people who had grown up with her around the cottage at the top of the Ruskey Road.

We didn't seem to realise that they had all been children a few decades earlier and had run and played in the Ruskey fields and along the lanes and had suddenly to be parted as young adults to go and find a new life far away from their own childhood haunts.

We just savoured the whole excitement of these moments as we got ready, waited on our mother who always put us first even at getting tidied up – and then sallied out together into the evening air. Although we went out nearly every evening it never lost its anticipated joy or its magic. We not only looked forward to meeting the same relatives and friends again, but we also couldn't wait to meet someone knew and interesting.

We couldn't wait to get out onto the cobbled yard in front of the cottage and dance and jump about until our mum came out as she was always last to get ready. Then, we would get on the move and along the rodden towards old Jane's cottage with her never ceasing ticking clock - or down to Davenports to visit my second godmother and midwife – Wee Mary.

Even to this day, I can recall minute details of that amazing, uneducated - but oh so wordly wise little woman. Her education in midwifery was gained without books, but in the harsh reality of having to learn her life - saving skills from other older women and through wonderful but at times bitter experience. Wee Mary, with her shortened, walking stick, her beguiling smile and her quiet words of wisdom, loved to see us coming along towards the house. We knew that she always sat outside on her wobbly stool, listening for the sounds of our shouts and singing – knowing that we always brought her some of her favourite sweets from Maggie's shop or

Wee Mary and my mother, the two most important women in my life. Wee Mary not only brought me into the world safely in my Inishowen cottage, but tended to my mother in the difficult days and weeks after my birth.

Michael's van. I can even remember the pattern of blue and yellow lines on the apron she seemed to wear everyday, but which still looked spotlessly clean no matter when or where you met her.

Although we set out to go and visit particular houses, especially if we knew they had relatives staying with them from America or England, we could suddenly end up in a totally different house and be there until the first streaks of dawn began to light up the sky.

Music was always in the air and my sister Bridget kept humming and repeating the words of her wide repertoire of songs over and over again. Her eyes sparkled and her heart beat swiftly as her excitement grew - knowing that we were on our way. We both wondered would it be to Mannie's or Katie and Sadie's or Kathleen and Philomena Barr or to Tilly's down at the main road at Whitecastle ? We just allowed ourselves to be swept along, delighted to enjoy once again the lovely songs and stories among our people and hills of Inishowen.

I was always amazed at how laid back and calm Bridget was about going out to visit local houses. Back home in Glasgow, she was a quiet, shy girl, but she never seemed in the slightest put out or uneasy about who she might meet or what might happen once she was in Inishowen. But then Bridget was totally at home in Inishowen – in the houses and hills and in the whole atmosphere of the singing and story telling. She absorbed everything with delight – the singing, the long discussions, the news about local events.

She listened in awe especially to all the tales of our own ancestors who had built the old house in the field at the top of the lane. She loved to hear over and over again that they had then actually carried the stones from the old house to help my grandparents as a newly married young couple build their own new cottage – the one where I was born and my mother and her brothers and sisters.

Although I loved the magic of our evening visits, I used to try to stay back in her shadow and anxiously wait until eventually someone would ask me to recite a poem from one of the books I was studying now that I was at Secondary school. I loved it as we moved from house to house; always feeling welcome no matter how many times we arrived and I soaked in the atmosphere and the people and left the singing to my much braver – and much more popular and gifted younger sister.

She had a natural, beautiful voice and as we travelled around the houses, she not only listened with delight, but added so much herself to the lives of the people she met - and they appreciated it with loud and generous applause. Everywhere we went, she would be asked to sing – over and over again. Of course it was a two - way love affair as Bridget's Scottish repertoire enthralled our neighbours as they longed to hear of the glens and lochs of Scotland.

It quite amazes me even now how much importance we put then on going out on our visits on those distant golden days in Donegal. I certainly remember it was one of the things we missed most when we eventually went back to our tenement life in Glasgow. When the long, drab winter evenings closed in around us, we craved for the pleasures of one evening around the turf fire on a warm, moonlit summer night - as the songs echoed out along our Inishowen hills - and down the fields towards the glistening shores of our beloved Loch Foyle.

Diary: August 14th : Sarah's Song

I really liked this song that I heard up in
Mannie's house last night. Mannie is mammy's cousin.
Sarah was singing the song and she called it Cottage by The Lea.
Here is what I remember of it and I think it's my favourite of all the
songs.

COTTAGE BY THE LEA

Tis well I know that often folk keep wondering,
when in my eyes a far off look they see.
What can it be , the cause of all my dreaming ?
What is this dream so very dear to me ?
YES, this is my dream, my lovely dream of homeland

And down the lane that runs behind the garden,
The blackbird greets the smiling summer morn.
And as his music echoes o'er the valley,
I smile and bless the day that I was born.

Notes:

Sarah is one of my favourite cousins and I liked the song best when
she sang the last verse. She actually sang it twice at the end and she is
always telling us to be thankful to God for being Irish - and happy
and healthy. We know that he brother Sam isn't very well just now
with a bad chest infection.

Chapter 16

Songs Across The Waters

Looking across the waters to County Derry, Antrim and towards Scotland.
Our songs and culture will always echo across The Foyle and bring us closer together.

Although we were totally absorbed in the lives and stories and events of our Inishowen hills, we were constantly being reminded of our Scots Connections. When we went into our Ruskey cottages and farms on our visits our main desire was to be enthralled by the voices and sounds and everyday events of our neighbours and friends. We listened in awe as they talked about all their everyday chores and happenings and, although to them many of these things were ordinary and had to be done, we found pleasure and excitement in the simplest activities and events of their daily lives.

Many a time they must have been irritated as we followed them in and out of the kitchen to feed chickens or go down to the well or take tea down to the workers in the hay field. But to our delight and childish joy, they always put up with us with patience and at times mild amusement.

We were quite delighted however at how often on our visits on the lovely summer evenings and often during the working day, we were asked about Glasgow and Scotland and all sorts of connections came into our happy discussions.

In our own cottage, Aunt Liza was always fiercely proud - and talked endlessly about the years she spent in Glasgow, particularly her days as a manageress in one of the busiest cinemas in Glasgow at Govan Cross. She often regaled us with her own stories of those days in her twenties when she had to evict noisy filmgoers and try to catch the youngsters who were being helped to 'skip in' by their friends without paying at the front kiosk.

She made us all laugh as she described in detail the schemes her young cinema patrons would get up to get their friends in for nothing. It was herself she boasted who worked out that they would slip down to the toilet in the dark and open one of the side doors to let their pals in and then return together to their seats. She was proud to boast to us too that she personally worked out a way to trap the ' mischeevious little scallywags ' as she called them.

She suggested to the manager that one of the lights was linked up to the door leading down to the toilets. As she pointed out in her dramatic way, unknown to the swashbuckling young intruders, the minute the side door was opened, the light above the main door would flash off and on, alerting her to anyone sneaking in without payment. It was easy then, she told us proudly, to wait and ambush the youngsters and catch them in the very act of their illegal entry in their eagerness to watch a Western or Tarzan movie.

Uncle Dan, my mother's brother, would also often regale us with his tales of working in the Glasgow Docks and his attempts to stop smuggling and pilfering from the array of warehouses which ran along the length of the Clydeside docks - from the Broomielaw to Finnieston. A teetotaller himself, he would have us laughing at the varied and mostly unsuccessful attempts by dock workers to gain entry to where the crates of whisky were stored - and their futile attempts to slip the odd bottle of whisky up the trouser legs of their baggy dungarees or in a bag of shipworker's tools.

Of course, Scotland was where my mother and father met, although both of them had been born in different parts of Ireland – my mother in Donegal and my father in Connemara.

It was no wonder then that with so many family connections to Scotland in our own cottage and in the houses of our neighbours, that there was a thirst for anything Scottish – especially stories and songs. Although we didn't realise it at the time, we were in a way little ambassadors for Scotland - and Bridget in particular never let anyone down.

As we moved from house to house, she would join in with all the singing of the Irish songs she loved so well herself – *My Lovely Irish Rose, The Rose of Tralee, The Hills of Donegal* and particularly the sad and brooding strains of *The Rose of Moray.*

I always remember trying to write down the words of some of our own Scottish songs, ones we were asked for over and over again. It always puzzled me at that age why there was such an interest in Scottish lochs and hills and particularly the poems of Robert Burns and his songs. I know now it was something within us Celts that linked us not just in name, but in culture and history to a shared love for the hills and glens and lochs and braes

Probably the most popular song that our Inishowen friends and neighbours like to hear Bridget singing, was *By Yon Bonnie Banks,* and knowing that they loved to hear a selection of Scottish songs, Bridget learned a medley that was always welcomed, and somehow touched a chord among everyone in the cottage.

She would usually start with a selection like the one I have written down in the next pages - and at times would stop and let me give a brief, sometimes very brief few words on something about the song, and the places mentioned. After we had been there a couple of weeks, encouraged by Bridget and desperate to show that I could make some contribution to the evenings entertainment, I would use some of the knowledge I had gained at home and especially from a Scottish history project we had just finished at school back in Glasgow.

Golden Days in Donegal

Here is a selection of what I remember Bridget singing and me trying to give some childish interpretations of what the songs were about

> By yon bonnie banks
> And by yon bonnie brae,
> where the sun shines bright on Ben Lomond.
> Where me and my true love
> Will ever wont tae gae,
> On the bonny , bonny banks of Loch Lomond.

> T'was there that we parted
> in yon shady glen,
> by the steep, steep sides of Ben Lomond.
> And me and my true love will never meet again,
> On the bonny, bonny banks of Loch Lomond.

> So you tak the high road,
> An' I'll tak the low road.
> 'n I'll be in Scotland afore ye.
> Then me an' my true love
> Will always ever meet
> On the bonny, bonny banks of Loch Lomond.

Bridget would then go into her medley with some of the following song, not always in this order and often making her own personal changes to the words when she couldn't exactly remember them properly.

> Roamin' in the gloaming
> On the bonny banks o' Clyde.
> Roamin' in the gloaming wae a laddie by ma side.
> When the sun has gone tae rest,
> That's the time that I like best.
> Oh it's lovely roamin' in the gloaming.
> Ah luv a laddie, a bonny bonny laddie.
> He's as true as the heather in the glen.
> He's as as true as the heather,
> the bonny, bloomin' heather.
> Hughie,
> ma true Scotsman.

Golden Days in Donegal

A favourite song that Bridget knew that all our Donegal relatives and friends loved was a wee popular song by a man called Harry Lauder. It was called *Stoap yir ticklin Joak*. This kind of silly song would always bring her medley to a close with loud clapping and laughter. That made her very happy to see everyone so delighted. This was Bridget's version of the song .

Wid ye stoap yir ticklin Joak?

Wid ye stoap yir ticklin Joak ?

Ah. Dinnae mak me laf sae herty,

Or ye'll mak me choak.

Wid ye stoap this tickilin Joak, jist look at aw the folk.

Wid ye stoap yir tickilin,

Tick –a lick – a – lickilin

STOAP

yir tickilin

JOAK !!

It never occurred to us at these times that our patient neighbours and their families had to be up at the crack of dawn and out milking or into the fields to catch the best of the improving Summer weather. But I still remember being asked so many questions as more turf was thown onto the fire and tea and scones were handed round and we all sat going over the songs and the words and the sounds.

I remember that our friends and neighbours loved to hear us speaking some of the words from the songs that were in Scottish, and always liked to hear us reciting the words of the Scottish songs or poems we had learned at school.

That was much easier for me, as singing was Bridget's forte and I can recall with great delight the farmers reactions as I rattled out words from poems which had become second nature to me through having to learn them off by heart for exams at school.

In particular, the poems of Robert Burns were always being asked for.

Uncle Johnnie, in his inimical, devilish way would put down his melodian and loudly let everyone know how pleased I would be to recite some poems. He would nip down to the lower room and bring up one of the high backed dinner chairs and sit it smack in front of the turf fire, so that I was visible to everyone in the room.

And then I would launch straight into my memorised poems, growing stronger in confidence as the poems went on and ending up swinging my hands and gesticulating to emphasise the famous words - much to the amusement of anyone who was listening.
A poem called *The Cottar's Saturday Night* was a favourite one, obviously striking a chord in the hearts of my weather beaten Inishowen relatives and friends. They could clearly identify with the wind and rain and darkness of similar nights in the middle of winter as the winds howled down from the Crehenan and Glencaw hills.

Here it is as I recall trying to do my best to capture the mood of the poem and the actions of my teacher back in Glasgow.

November chill blaws loud wi angry sughhhhhhhhhhhhh
The short'ning winter day is near a close;
The miry beasts retreatin' frae the plough;
The black'ning trains o craws to their repose.

AYE. It's in this kind of nicht,
the toil - worn Cotter frae his labor goes.
This Night – This Nicht – This very Nicht,
his weekly toil is at an end
'n he collects his spades, his mattocks and his hoes,
hoping the morn in ease and rest to spend.
'N weary, ...weary ...weary,
O'er the moor
his course does hameward bend.

The other Burns poem that I remember they loved so much - and which usually brought peels of sympathetic laughter, had nothing to do with the toils and weary plodding back through the hills to the cottage on a wild, wintry night.

This poem, called *To A Mouse*, told the simple tale of Burns coming across a mouse when he was out cutting hay. The accidental wrecking of the mouse's nest was an event of no importance whatsoever. I soon realised from their reactions that the farmers and fieldworkers of Inishowen would have paid as little attention as a Scottish farmer to such an everyday, minor event in the hard slog of cutting, binding, stacking and bringing in the hay.

I think what appealed to them so much though was that Burns – an ordinary cottager himself - could write so passionately and so affectionately about this insignificant little field mouse. As usual our neighbours and friends and especially Aunt Liza loved the fact that they knew I would put on a stronger than natural Scotch accent, mixed in with my own Glasgow dialect as I recited the poem. They also knew that, at times, I would only remember my own version of the poem, as I revelled in my only real chance of glory around the turf fire in my Donegal cottage.

Often, as I would go into my recitations, I would start shuffling about in between the people in the cottage that night. In and out and around tables and chairs - as if fumbling for the mouse on the hearth floor.

Tae a moose

Wee, sleekit, coowrin, timoorus beastie,
O, whit a panic 's in thy breastie !
Ye needni stert awa sae hasty,
Wi' bickerin' brattle.
Ah wid be laith
tae rin 'n chase thee,
Wi' murderin pattle.

Yir wee bit hoosie , tae, in ruin.
It's silly wa's tae the wind are strewin.
Ye saw the fields laid bare 'n waste,
'n weary winter cumin fast.
'n cozie here,
ye thocht tae dwell,
beneath the blast.
' Till craaaaaaaaaaash.
The cruel coulter
cut richt through yir cell.

I always tried to stop at this point and show off a bit, trying to explain some of Burn's words, like *sleekit, brattle, pattle* - and trying to see if they had ever heard these Scots words before. As they laughed and joked and urged me on, understanding full well the simple meaning of the poem, I always tried to finish with a flourish, remembering my English teacher's dramatic statements in class that Burns wanted to make a big prophetic human message with such *a simple poem*.

Although I never really understood the great significance of Burn's prophecies in his writings about the fultility of life and the dread of the future, I can remember drawing in my breath and glancing round, trying to delay the final pessimistic punch lines that Burns finished the poem with.

I would usually jump up a bit and throw my arms out in mock despair:

> *'But mousie,'*
> I would shout out:
> *' Thou art no yir lane,*
> *In provin' foresight may be vain.*
> *Aye, the best laid plans o' mice an men*
> *Gang aft Agley.*
> *an lea us nocht but grief an pain,*
> *for promised joys.*
> *Still thou art blest, compar'd wi ME !*
> *The present only touches thee :*
> *But Och !*
> *I backwards cast my e'e,*
> *An forward,*
> *tho ah canna see-*
> *Ah guess –*
>
> *an Fear !'*

As our Summer days in Donegal passed from one glorious memory to another, we never failed to enjoy our evenings of song and poem. We also hoped desperately that we could bring some new pleasure to our own relatives and friends - as we shared the songs and stories and poems of our precious Celtic culture.

Even at that young age, we felt that there were magical bonds and connections - through our families and in the events of our lives - that drew us closer and closer together. We never lost these bonds and could relish the memory of them often, whether we were in our beloved Donegal hills and fields - or longing to get back to our cottage from the busy, bustling streets of Glasgow.

Courtesy Inish Times

Chapter 17

Sunset on The Foyle

Golden, lingering sunsets on the Foyle were something we never tired of watching. As our long summer days drew slowly to a close and the river and our beloved hills were bathed in the last rays of the sun, we sat for ages to admire and savour the close of day. We watched enthralled from many of our favourite places along the Foyle, especially coming up from Moville or Drung, usually weary, but happy as the evening closed in.

My own favourite spot was sitting cross legged on the huge boulder at the back of the lane behind the cottage. From there, I could catch the last faint heat of the sun's rays and watch it slowly but inevitably dip down behind Glencaw Hill with Slieve Snacht away in the distance. As the fields grew hazy and the distant voices in the fields died away in the late evening air, I had a special feeling of being somehow part of the people and the landscape in front of me – something I had never experienced back in Glasgow.

The only time however when sunset on the Foyle lost any of its magic was on the evening we made our return journey down the Foyle on our way back to Glasgow after our long, glorious school holidays. Going back to Glasgow was something we tried not to think about, and packed as much into the last few days in Inishowen as we could. We got up even earlier. We fitted in even more visits and games and journeys as we could, and we squeezed every extra moment of pleasure we could into our summer lives in the fields, roads and houses of our Donegal hills.

Of course, whether we liked it or not, the days and the glorious weeks passed. The dreaded reality eventually overwhelmed us that we would soon have to go back to Glasgow and back to school. Most of the time, as we played and ran about and enjoyed the best of everything in our idyllic Donegal world, the thought of having to leave it all – even for a short time – crept uneasily into our minds. Bridget was always someone for keeping diaries and lovingly noted down names and places and events. I had, as many boys naturally do, abandoned the routine of keeping my diary as I became totally engrossed in everything that we took part in. I eventually abandoned my good intentions to write things down. But the one date Bridget never put down, and tried to avoid at all costs, was the day that we knew all this summer magic would come to an end.

We didn't have any return tickets booked and that helped us to keep the date of our eventual departure as vague and as hidden in our minds as we could. We knew, however, that at some time we would have to face the reality, especially when our mother, in her quiet, supportive way would drop little hints that we should think about saying some early goodbye's - especially to any of our family and friends and neighbours furthest away from our Ruskey Cottage – in Moville and Muff and up the Carn brae.

Of course we never talked about going back to Scotland and kept it to the back of our minds. As we raced along the lower fields and down to our friends' houses, we often saw the Lairds Loch majestically heading down the Foyle, but we were just glad that we weren't on it. We could sit back for a while on a dyke at the entrance to Mary Rose's fields or on the edge of a wall at Sam Mullan's - overlooking the Foyle, and enjoy the sight of the ship ploughing its way down past Whitecastle Light, out towards Redcastle Buoy and into the deeper channel that would take it down past Moville.

We could just make out the outlines of passengers, some wandering along the deck, others standing at the rails, clustered together we felt in little groups to talk and ease the thought of being so near – and yet so far – from the land they loved. We felt moments of sadness for them too, knowing that many of them were casting last, sad glances back towards the shore and their family and friends until they could be back the following year. In those days most of us hadn't the luxury of coming back at the October holidays or at Christmas or Easter. Most of us had that one glorious summer holiday. Probably the only other times people came back was if someone in the family took ill or died or perhaps for a special family event like a wedding or Christening.

But looking down from our safe haven in the hills, we could see some of them waving towards the lonely hillside cottages - and the fires and white sheets flying in the wind - as the loved ones they had left behind tried to make their Foyle departure as painless as possible. As the captain gave sympathetic blasts on the ship's siren, trying to acknowledge the fires or white sheets or people on the shore, we felt that even the old Lairds Loch herself was trying to make it easier for her despondent passengers.

As the 'Scotch Boat' gradually sailed out of sight and away down past Greencastle and over towards the Antrim Coast, we cast a last, uneasy glance at it and then escaped as fast as we could back into our wonderland of friends and families and Inishowen fantasies.

But despite our attempts to hide from this impending blot on our idyllic landscape and summer wonderland, the dreaded day for leaving crept up with relentless, ever increasing speed. At the start of our holidays, we could always console ourselves with the delirious joy that it would be weeks and weeks before any thoughts of going back began to haunt us at night.

However, we always felt the time beginning to race forward after our last Sunday Mass down at St Columba's in Drung. Unsettling thoughts would start to drift into our minds, especially when Dr McGurk would remark on 'the small numbers of Scotch visitors at today's Mass' or when we went down to Drung afterwards and found out that many of our friend's relatives had already headed back to Scotland or England.

So when the eventual dreaded day came and we could no longer prolong our golden days, we resigned ourselves reluctantly to helping our mother get everything ready for the journey back up to Derry. I remember that year that our sadness at going back to Glasgow was eased a little by my mother making sure that Neil Smith would be hired to take us back up the lower road. She knew in her own way that we had no real right after all those weeks to be depressed - that we were in fact going 'home' to our dad and our brothers Martin and Paddy. But, having felt the pangs herself on leaving her parents years before and having to go through the agony of leaving her own Inishowen family and friends, she understood our childish sadness. As usual in her own quiet way, she did anything she could to get us ready for the journey to the quayside in Derry.

Aunt Liza and Uncle Johnnie as well, despite having had us there in their two roomed cottage for two long, busy summer months, sensed our unease and made extra efforts to make our last few days fuller and even more enjoyable. As the weather fortunately remained glorious, we were allowed more opportunities to go with them herding the cattle or collecting precious eggs which the hens had laid in bushes and mosses behind the cottage. Uncle Johnnie even allowed us both the extreme privilege of cycling on our own, unsupervised up to the Crossroads and along the upper road to Mannie's Rooskey Cottage. We were absolutely delighted when he then agreed that we could return the long way, down the lower Ruskey Road to the corner where Old Jane and Bridget Armstrong lived - and then back along the bumpy, dusty rodden to our own cottage. We were only too happy then to take our turns, over and over again and to please uncle Johnnie by fetching and carrying extra buckets of water up from the river to wash down his beloved bicycle at the end of our bonus trips.

Our last evening came inevitably and we went round as many of our neighbour's houses as we could, this time on shorter, more subdued visits. As usual they did all they could to make the break as easy as possible. Most of our own talk in houses that evening was about our return to Donegal, maybe, Bridget hoped fervently, at Christmas or at Easter. We talked all the time about how we would recall and boast to our Glasgow friends about all the adventures we had - and all the friends and beautiful memories we had taken home with us.

When the day came and Neil Smith's horn sounded at the foot of the lane, we said hurried goodbyes and tried to show our mother that we would rise out of our self pity and make her journey back to Glasgow as pleasant as possible. Her health was still not good and although the break amongst her own people and hills had revived her strength and brought colour to her cheeks, we felt that after all the joys we had experienced we should now make sure that she was number one. And we would take her back to Glasgow and share our glorious memories with her and make her feel that all the efforts she had made to get us over for the summer months were worthwhile.

So the departure from our cottage that day was always a symbolic, momentous event. All the glorious days we had spent since the first day we came up Lough Foyle seemed to give us strength of mind and purpose for the farewells. But, as Neil loaded up the boot with our bags and cases and we slumped down in the back of the car, no matter how hard we tried to smile and appear positive, somehow we didn't experience the same feelings of luxury or magic that had so enthralled us the previous time we had scrambled into his Cadillac at the Derry Quay. But as Neil sped away from the cottage, down the Ruskey Road and headed up towards Quigley's Point, we drew closer as a family, knowing that our golden days had bonded us even closer together.

The journey up the first part of the road to Derry seemed un - naturally long, almost as if Neil was giving us a last chance to catch a glimpse of all the places where we had spent so many happy days – along past the wee cottage at the foot of the Crehenan Road and up past the cliff cottage – half way up to Quigley's Point.

And then as Neil slowed down through the village, we caught a glimpse of McKeever's shop and our friends waving outside Callaghan's Hotel. And there was Michael tidying out his mobile shop for his run the next day up through the hills - to the cottages and farms we would not be seeing for many long days and nights. The shore - field was empty now where the Sports had been held and where Charlie Grant's Mare had stolen the show and where I chased Anna around the haystacks and down towards the beach. But my mother, sensing how we were only making our departing agony worse, must have given Neil a nod or a slight dunt, as he suddenly revved up and the car sped out of the village and along past Greenbank Hall. Before we knew it we were racing past Ture and round the long sweeping bend that would take us though Muff, Culmore and then on into Derry.

As we arrived early at the quayside, Neil, in his usual calm, efficient way, got as close to the Lairds Loch as he could and helped us up the gangway, along the deck and down the giant stairs that took us to the seats where we would spend the night. We got good seats and lifejackets and a position near the middle of the ship where it was most comfortable and less bumpy if the crossing was in any way rough.

But we were in luck again - and the evening was calm and bright and the sinking sun gave a warm glow to us on the stern of the old ship as she eased her way once again away from the quayside and down towards Culmore Light.

Derry was in her evening attire now, as she had been in a dawn slumber when we arrived those long glorious weeks before. But we were oblivious to the crowds of passengers returning home that night and my sister Bridget and I stood on the deck for the whole journey down the river – totally engrossed in our final views of the shore and the lower road and the cottages and houses we were leaving for another year.

As the Lairds Loch gathered speed down past Whitecastle light, the captain gave a long, lingering blast on the ship's siren and we gazed up past Whitecastle House on our beloved shore and up the Ruskey Road. We could clearly make out the white sheets billowing out along the rodden as Aunt Liza and Uncle Johnnie said farewell in their own personal way. To my disappointment, I had forgotten the old binoculars that I had used so enthusiastically to view almost every landmark on the way up the Foyle the day we had arrived.

But in its own way, it was better that I had forgotten or mislaid them, for as the ship glided down the river past Moville and out towards the Antrim Coast, we had seen enough and made our way slowly back along the ship towards where we had organised our home for the night. As we turned to take our last look back up the Foyle, the sun broke out from the lowest clouds away behind us - and a glorious sunset cast an enchanting warm glow all across The Foyle Derry and our Inishowen hills.   At that moment, we accepted that we were now on our way out of our Donegal paradise. We both sadly turned our backs on the distant hills and went swiftly down to our mother where we would spend the rest of the night. With our seats secure and our beds set out, we settled down to be together and started making our plans to come back to our holiday haven in Donegal as soon as we could.

We knew that in our minds we held the key to reliving our days of joy. We knew that we alone held all the beautiful memories of our Inishowen summer - and consoled ourselves that we could recall the happiness of our golden days - over and over again. We knew that these beautiful memories would be with us until we came back again to revel in the wonder of a new, welcoming dawn - a dawn that would bring us joyfully back up Lough Foyle to our beloved people, cottages and hills of Inishowen.